THE VENETO
VENICE TO THE DOLOMITES

PHILIP'S TRAVEL GUIDES

THE VENETO
VENICE TO THE DOLOMITES

STEPHEN BROOK

PHOTOGRAPHY BY JOE CORNISH

GEORGE
PHILIP

British Library Cataloguing in Publication Data

Brook, Stephen *1947–*
    The Veneto.—(Philip's travel guides).
    1. Italy.   Veneto—Visitors' guides
    I. Title
    914.5304929

ISBN 0–540–01232–7

Text © Stephen Brook 1991
Photographs © Joe Cornish 1991
Maps © George Philip 1991

First published by George Philip Limited,
59 Grosvenor Street, London W1X 9DA

Printed in Italy

Contents

Acknowledgements

I should like to thank Anselmo Centomo of Azienda Promozione Turistica Vicenza and Contessa Francesca Giusti del Giardino Piovene for making it possible for me to visit some of the villas of the Veneto. Two great winemakers, Roberto Anselmi and Nino Franceschetti, were generous with information and hospitality. As always, the support of my wife Maria, both logistical and moral, proved invaluable.

Half-title illustration **Art and nature in harmony at the church of San Giorgio in the Valpolicella area.**

Title-page illustration **In a valley of the Dolomites, the village of Alleghe cowers beneath Monte Civetta.**

Opposite **Flowers on stone at Torri del Benaco: a constant motif in the mild climate of Lake Garda.**

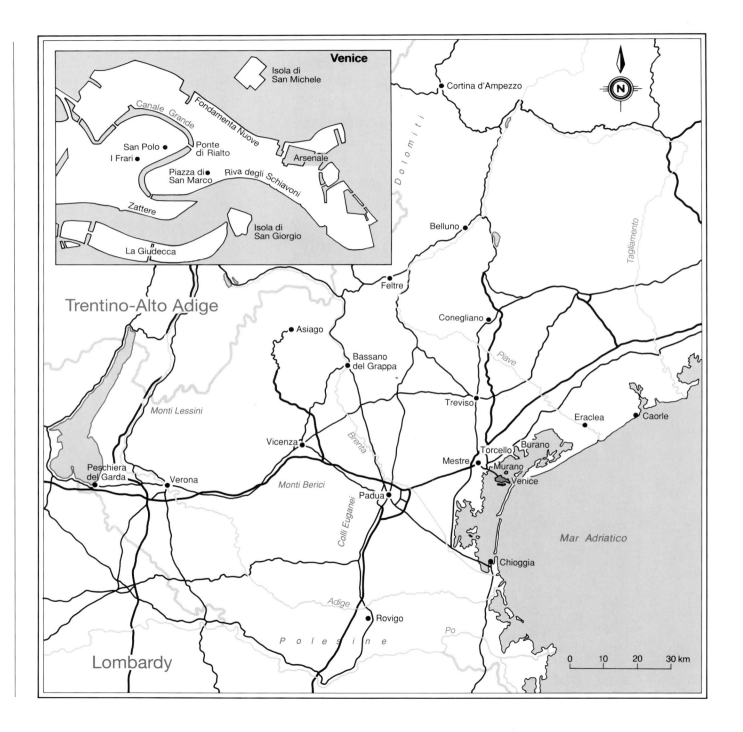

Venice

Isola di
San Michele

Canale Grande

Fondamenta Nuove

San Polo
I Frari
Ponte
di Rialto
Piazza di
San Marco
Riva degli Schiavoni
Arsenale

Zattere

Isola di
San Giorgio

La Giudecca

Trentino-Alto Adige

Cortina d'Ampezzo

Dolomiti

Belluno

Tagliamento

Feltre

Conegliano

Piave

Asiago

Bassano
del Grappa

Treviso

Eraclea

Caorle

Monti Lessini

Vicenza

Brenta

Torcello
Burano
Mestre
Murano
Venice

Peschiera
del Garda

Verona

Monti Berici

Colli Euganei

Padua

Mar Adriatico

Chioggia

Adige

Rovigo

Po

Polesine

Lombardy

0   10   20   30 km

Introduction

The Veneto and Venice. Two names springing from the same root. And indeed, the influence of Venice on the mainland region it once ruled has been considerable. From the fifteenth century onwards, the great water-threaded city on the lagoon controlled most of north-eastern Italy. The present-day *regione* of the Veneto does not include other areas, such as the Friuli north-east of Venice, which were once under Venice's rule. But it does include Verona, Treviso, Padua, Vicenza and many other cities where the emblem of Venetian rule, the winged lion of St Mark, remains ubiquitous.

Many of these cities are far more ancient than Venice itself, a relatively recent foundation. When Venice was no more than a succession of uninhabited water-logged islands in the lagoon, there were thriving ancient civilizations based around towns such as Este and Adria, cultures documented in those cities' archaeological museums. The Romans later transformed such settlements as Verona and Vicenza and Este into major cities, centres of trade and commerce. A series of barbarian invasions – the Huns in the fifth century, the Longobards two centuries later, and the Magyars two centuries after that in 899 – both wrecked the prosperity of the Veneto and induced many city dwellers to flee to the relative safety of the lagoon. Even then, it was not present-day Venice that was the principal site of settlement but the more northerly island of Torcello. Other islands, such as Burano and Mazzorbo, were also settled, as were the coastal towns of Chioggia, Eraclea, and Caorle.

The early inhabitants of the lagoon exploited both the commercial expertise they brought with them, and the unique strategic location of the waters they controlled, to build up a trading empire of increasing wealth and sophistication. More islands were colonized, and by the twelfth century *palazzi* were already lining the Grand Canal. With Venetian eyes trained eastwards on the Byzantine world and beyond, from which the city derived its immense prosperity, there was little inclination or need to pay much attention to the mainland. The early Middle Ages were, in any case, a period of fragmentation, with a succession of warlords ruling the major cities and indulging in military intrigues against their rivals. Some of these ruling families were tyrannical, others content to preside over city *comuni* that enjoyed considerable independence and cultural vigour.

Venice, facing the sea, nevertheless protected its back. The city aided the major cities of the Veneto in resisting the ambitions of Holy Roman Emperor Frederick Barbarossa (1155–90) in the twelfth century, and some cities were governed by an official known as the *podestà*, a kind of local governor dispatched from Venice. There was conflict too, and a war with Padua,

then rule by the Scaligeri clan, resulting in a peace treaty in 1339 that gave Venice itself, for the first time, control over cities to the north such as Conegliano and Treviso. The republican system under which Venice had thrived was transferred and adapted to its mainland cities. The councils that filled the Doge's Palace in Venice were duplicated, in less cumbersome form, in cities such as Treviso and Verona; these cities were granted considerable independence, although the *podestà*'s essential loyalty still lay with Venice itself.

The peace treaty did not, of course, keep the peace for long. Seventeen years later the Paduan warlord, Umberto da Carrara, flaunted his independence of Venice by siding with a powerful Hungarian challenge to the Veneto. The Venetians, having come to somewhat humiliating terms with the Hungarians, then turned their attention to Padua, and successfully crushed Da Carrara.

This instability continued through the latter part of the fourteenth century. Neighbouring cities such as Treviso, Chioggia and Padua were fought over. By the early fifteenth century, however, Venice had consolidated its control. Once troublesome Padua had been vanquished in 1404, Venice had a firm grip on most of the present-day region of the Veneto. There would be more skirmishing, as in 1411, when the cities of Feltre and Belluno were lost to Venice, but successfully recaptured nine years later; and in 1484 Venice expanded its holdings on the mainland when it acquired Rovigo and the Polesine region.

Venice's grip over the Veneto coincided with a shift in its economic fortunes. Throughout the Middle Ages Venice had thrived as a sea-trading nation. All its requirements, even grain, were imported. As long as Venice could maintain its control over the waterways of the Mediterranean, this state of affairs posed no problem. But from the fifteenth century onwards, its maritime position began to come under threat. Thus it became in Venice's own interest to develop what was

The Porta Ruga at Belluno, a city gate built under Venetian rule.

In Feltre, a covered stairway links the upper and lower parts of the old town.

known as 'terra firma'. Much of the mainland around the lagoon was low-lying and swampy and, from the 1520s onwards, these lands were drained and returned to agricultural use.

This colonization of the mainland did not mean that Venice had gained, together with its territorial expansion, any real security. During the early years of the sixteenth century the League of Cambrai, an alliance of papal and Habsburg interests, attempted to deal a fatal blow to Venetian power. Lands and cities were lost and regained as the struggle for the mainland continued from one year to the next. Venice was the ultimate victor, and the settling and agricultural exploitation of terra firma continued. At this time were built the majority of the great villas of the Veneto, designed so as to combine the functions of country retreat and working farm.

By the 1540s stability had returned, but later that century Venice would suffer both from the plague and

The elegant gothic portal of the Chiesetta della Natività at Thiene.

from military threats on its eastern front from the Turks. The Venetians were greatly buoyed up by the triumph against the Turks at the sea battle of Lepanto, but the process of decline was irreversible, and by 1718, with the peace of Passarowitz, Venice had in effect relinquished its claims to the eastern Mediterranean. The humiliation was completed in May 1797, when the last Doge, Lodovico Manin, handed the city over to Napoleon. The great city became a token of exchange between the French and the Austrian Habsburgs, who ruled until 1866 when Italy's independence was secured, and Venice became part of the new nation.

Although Venice retained its possessions on terra firma from the early sixteenth century until Napoleonic times, the cities and regions of the Veneto retained both a measure of governmental independence and considerable cultural independence. Despite such unifying characteristics as the presence of the winged lion on public buildings and the massive sixteenth-century fortifications constructed by the Venetians around cities such as Padua and Treviso and Peschiera, to travel through the Veneto is to experience variety as much as uniformity. Architectural styles, dialects, cuisine, all reflect local character. The Veneto is indeed Venetian, but it is much more than that.

Topographically, the region is somewhat confused, a consequence partly of historical development and partly of administrative dictum. To the north it includes part of the magnificent Dolomite range, while another portion of the same range lies within Trentino and the Alto Adige. North of Venice the border wriggles up towards Austria alongside that of another region, Friuli-Venezia Giulia, which historically has as great a claim to be part of the Veneto as do the Dolomites. But this topographical chaos provides the region with much of its interest, not only in the mountains themselves but to the north of the Veneto plains, where the distant Dolomites provide a constant and glittering backdrop. Nor are the plains that stretch westward from Venice to Verona and Lake Garda entirely without relief. South-west of Padua are the Colli Euganei, and south of Vicenza are the Monti Berici, gentle rolling hill country still steeped in a pastoral tranquillity that is absent from many other parts of the region.

Only in the south, along the border with Emilia-Romagna, is the landscape frankly dull. Here in the Polesine, the delta of the River Po, is an expansive region of marshes, flat fields, canals, and forbidding brick farm complexes. On a spring morning, when the birds are loud in the vast sky and fishermen nod over their rods along the waterways, the Polesine can be idyllic, but on a foggy wintry morning the great expanses can be thoroughly dispiriting.

There is, of course, far more to the Veneto than

Villa Cornaro at Piombino Dese: a masterly villa by Palladio asserts the Venetian domination of land as well as water.

landscape. Its cities are packed with architecture that includes some of Italy's greatest Roman monuments as well as an array of magnificent cathedrals and abbeys. Venice, with its wealth of commissions both religious and civic, encouraged the development of such marvellous painters as Carpaccio, Bellini, Titian, Tintoretto, Veronese and the Tiepolos, Giambattista and Giovanni Domenico, father and son. Other cities spawned their own artists – the Bassanos, Cima da Conegliano, Morto da Feltre, Canova, Brustolon – many of whom rapidly attained international fame. Vicenza is crammed with the palaces of Palladio and his follower Scamozzi. Their villas, and those of Sansovino and Sammicheli and countless other fine architects, are dotted across the Veneto, lovely stately houses in perfect harmony with the surrounding countryside. The work of lesser-known architects and designers such as the Lombardo family and Andrea Briosco is generously represented in the region, which is all the richer for it. The churches and cathedrals glow with the colours of frescoes by the likes of Giotto and Mantegna, Altichiero and Pisanello, Montagna and Zelotti. Venice, of course, is *sui generis*, with works by almost all the artists mentioned above, and the supreme masterpiece of its own evolution through time, its own unique topography.

The Veneto offers writers as diverse as Petrarch (1304–74), who spent his last years in the Colli Euganei, and the Venetian playwright Goldoni (1707–93). Its rulers have varied from the bland, curiously impotent Doges of Venice, backed by an imperial might they could rarely shape and control, to the heads of warring clans such as the Scaligeri, the Carraresi and the Visconti. From the fifteenth century, when Venetian domination of the region began and remained constant for three centuries, and control was exercised through officials such as the *podestà*, the bloodshed and strife of the medieval period – and, it must be admitted, the marvellous artistic achieve-

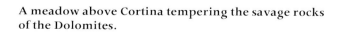
A meadow above Cortina tempering the savage rocks of the Dolomites.

The Venetian love of colour and ornament is lavished on exteriors as much as interiors, as this *palazzo* in Feltre demonstrates.

ments of those same bloody centuries – give way to a more tranquil and uneventful time which allowed the great institutions such as the church and the universities to flourish.

So whether one's primary interest is landscape or architecture or cityscape or brimming art galleries or good food and wine, the Veneto has a vast amount to offer. The Italian authorities have, for the most part, done a splendid job of preserving their beautiful cities. Cars are either banned from or under severe restrictions of movement within city centres. Large pedestrian precincts in cities such as Verona and Vicenza and Padua make it pleasurable to visit them. Plentiful hotels, restaurants, and highly efficient cafés offer welcome relief from the arduous business of sightseeing. In Rome I once had to clamber over a Fiat that entirely blocked a pavement; such measures are rarely necessary in the well-regulated cities of the Veneto.

A Dolomite inn at Pieve di Livignalongo.

The countryside, however, is a different matter. The southern part of the Veneto, with the exception of the small hilly areas to the south of Vicenza and Padua, is entirely flat. You must search hard for anything that an inhabitant of Britain, North America or France would recognize as countryside. Urban sprawl is ubiquitous, traffic congestion constant, new construction seemingly uncontrolled. Even where copses and fields make a hesitant appearance, the visitor's view of them is obstructed by the succession of hoardings and advertisements that are a constant eyesore along Italian roads. Only topography can defeat this blight; the roads of the Dolomites and other mountainous regions of the Veneto are mostly free of such excrescences, and of the innumerable industrial zones of the plain. But the mountains offer other hazards. Some of the passes around Cortina are narrow and tortuous, and the more remote ones, especially those whose primary function is military, are often closed. In mid April I once took what appeared on the map to be a perfectly negotiable pass from the Lessini mountains north of Verona into the Trentino, only to discover at the summit that the descent was a single-lane road that had not been ploughed all winter. The snow was still thick, but I managed to slither slowly down the icy ruts that passed for a road and kept praying that I wouldn't encounter another car on its way up. There had been no prior warning of these nightmarish conditions.

The pleasures of the Veneto are intense – a rich and varied cuisine, the loveliest mountains in Italy, and an artistic and cultural heritage unsurpassed in Europe – but there are times when the enjoyment of that *patrimonio* can seem quite a struggle.

Some of the most valued ingredients of north Italian cooking are grown in the Veneto, such as radicchio from around Treviso and asparagus from Bassano. Chioggia is famous for its cuttle-fish (*seppie*) and crabs, Asiago and its mountain plateau for a soft-textured cheese. A number of famous dishes are associated with the region: *risi e bisi*, a hefty Venetian soup of bacon, peas, onions and rice; *fegato alla veneziana*, finely sliced calves' liver cooked with butter and onions; *baccalà mantecato*, a creamed salt cod dish not unlike the French *brandade de morue*; *baccalà alla vicentina*, a braised stewed version of the same fish from Vicenza, pungent with anchovies and garlic; roasted rabbit (*coniglio*); the wholewheat spaghetti called *bigoli*; and the ubiquitous *polenta*, which is simply boiled maize flour which is then fried or baked or toasted and served in place of rice or potatoes. I find that a very little *polenta* goes a very long way, and am at a loss to understand the north Italian addiction to the leaden stuff. Far more interesting is *risotto*, not of course a dish restricted to the Veneto, though combined here with all manner of local ingredients. In winter try the Veronan Christmas speciality *pandoro*, a tall and very light sponge cake. But most exquisite of all, surely, is the seafood, the prawns and mussels and crabs and cuttle-fish and all the other wondrous creatures that crawl across the bed of the lagoon and shuffle along the Adriatic shore.

For some reason, good food, unless price is no object,

is most difficult to find in Venice itself. The smart restaurants are ludicrously overpriced, and on the few occasions when I have eaten in them, there have been irritating lapses, such as oversalted dishes or problems with wine waiters trying to pass off oxidized bottles as perfectly drinkable. Nor have I had better luck in the neighbourhood *trattorie* in Canareggio and other corners of Venice less frequented by tourists. For the most part, the food there has been miserable. Restaurants are said to be good in Mestre, just across the causeway on the mainland, but that does not seem a sufficient reason to plunge into the urban confusions and industrial aromas of that city. Seafood, such as the local specialities *moleche* (small soft-shell crabs) and the large crabs known as *grancevole* or *granceole*, are probably better, and less expensive, in Burano or Chioggia or Caorle.

Venice may not be the ideal place to sample the region's gastronomy, but, as visitors have been discovering for a thousand years, it does have a few other things to offer by way of compensation. Despite all the ravages of decay and pollution, its beauty and the unique light of the lagoon remain unimpaired. So plentiful are the beauties of the city – its hundreds of ancient *palazzi*, its dozens of splendid churches and squares, and its unique aquatic character – that even the decaying condition of many of them seems part of the urban furniture. Venice, despite or because of its undeniable freakishness, is a city of dreams and fantasies, too astounding to be entirely rooted in reality. Byron, in a memorable phrase, referred to it as 'the greenest island of my imagination'. Venice is too large, too complex to be prettified; no restoration programme can ever do more than scratch the surface of a city that in its totality is simultaneously a work of art and a home.

To enjoy the city, you must first shock yourself by an initial exposure, then immerse yourself in it. To be dazzled by Venice is not a novel experience. In the early seventeenth century, travellers such as Thomas Coryate were raving in their notebooks about 'this incomparable city, this most beautifull Queene, this untainted virgine, this Paradise, this Tempe, this rich Diademe and most flourishing garland of Christendome'. By the late 1800s, even experienced and articulate travellers such as Henry James were having difficulty adding to the encomiums of the centuries: 'There is nothing new to be said about [Venice] certainly, but the old is better than any novelty.' What is new, sadly, since the time when James was writing, is the impact of the environment on this delicately balanced city. In this respect it is subject to many of the problems that beset other parts of the Veneto. Pollution from Mestre and other industrial cities on the mainland, a declining population, and a reluctance to control the influx of tourists, so generously equipped with dollars and Deutschmarks, that overrun Venice in summer, give the city a permanent headache.

It is best, if time permits, not to treat the city solely as a living museum, for to dash from church to palace is to experience only part of Venice. It is equally important to linger over a grappa in a bar along the Zattere, to lean over the bridges and watch the water traffic, to relish the changes in the light at dusk, when the lagoon is surely at its most magical, to stand in a *traghetto*, or gondola ferry, crossing the Grand Canal, to watch as a wedding party moves luxuriantly through the canals from church to restaurant. Above all, it is hard to experience Venice until you have become lost here, especially at night. A wrong turn can lead through a silent alley to the brink of a canal; the howl of a cat can terrify you as you hear your steps echo down a deserted path; the shuttered houses will remind you of the vast gap between resident and visitor.

For such pleasures and experiences there can be no programme. And it is surely a mistake to act too ravenously when approaching the beauties of Venice. Take heed of Mark Twain's ironic words in *The Innocents Abroad* (1869):

We have seen thirteen thousand St Jeromes, and twenty-two thousand St Marks, and sixteen thousand St Matthews, and sixty thousand St Sebastians, and four millions of assorted monks, undesignated, and we feel encouraged to believe that when we have seen some more of these various pictures, and had a larger experience, we shall begin to take an absorbing interest in them like our cultivated countrymen.

It is for each individual to expose himself or herself to those experiences which will become memorable and encapsulating. This book, which makes no claim to be a substitute for the many excellent guide books to Venice, can do no more than point the visitor to some of the sights that are instructive because of their symbolic as well as aesthetic power, and mention a handful of those spots in the city that mean the most to its author.

Walk into the great Piazza di San Marco, and the initial impression, it always seems to me, is not of the byzantine splendour of the basilica in front of you, but of the unsurpassed urbanity of the whole: the ranges of arcaded civic buildings along three sides of the square, all of different architectural styles and yet unified by time and familiarity, the smart shops and elegant cafés beneath them, and then the vast yet unceremonial space of the piazza itself, traversed by all, native and tourist, crook and priest, child and dotard. This civilized expanse is watched over, from the clock-tower to the right and from the central gable of the basilica, by the winged lion of St Mark, the symbol of Venice. We see it again on the wing of the Doge's palace facing the Piazzetta, this time in the company of Doge Foscari.

It's hard to avoid stepping into San Marco on coming upon it for the first time, but a thorough exploration should be reserved, if time permits, for a later stage during one's visit. The basilica is so rich, so overwhelming, that it can appear crushing and un-readable. By visiting other churches and monuments and thereby acquiring some grasp of the disparate historical and artistic elements that converged and developed in Venice, you will find St Mark's more manageable and more interesting. It is, of course, a byzantine church: its floors, its capitals, its domes, and above all its mosaics make this abundantly clear. This is medieval Venice at its most glorious and mystical. In the piazza and adjoining Piazzetta, and in the interior

of the Doge's Palace, we see the Venetian Renaissance, but here we are in the presence of the almost barbarous splendour of Venice's earlier history. It reminds us forcibly of the Serenissima's links with the east, of the days of the empire's greatest expansion, when a Marco Polo could travel as far as China and back. Sansovino's bronzes and bronze sacristy door, the fourteenth-century iconostasis statues, the massive pulpits, the fabulous Pala d'Oro in the choir, the gothic tomb of Andrea Dandolo (1307–54) in the baptistery, the fabulous mosaics: there's matter enough to fill days of exploration and contemplation, so the basilica is better appreciated in morsels than in one great bite.

On leaving the church turn left towards the entrance to the Doge's Palace for evidence of how many of Venice's treasures were the fruits of conquest and rapacity. The fourth-century bronze horses (those actually on the parapet of the basilica are, alas, copies) were stolen, as were many of the pillars and carvings found here near the Piazzetta. The most alluring piece of plunder is probably the group of fourth-century Egyptian porphyry figures huddled apprehensively on the corner between the south entrance to San Marco and the entrance to the Doge's Palace.

To understand what Venice meant, in terms of its power and influence and self-regard, and how it perceived itself, it is essential to visit the palace. As you climb the great double staircase to the upper floor, you are passing beneath the handiwork of two of the city's great designers: Jacopo Sansovino (1467/71–1529) and Alessandro Vittoria (1525–1608). Sansovino created the immense renaissance library on the other side of the Piazzetta, which Palladio (1508–80), the most celebrated architect of the Veneto, himself applauded as the greatest building since those of Roman antiquity on which it was modelled, and the more playful Loggietta at the base of the campanile. Vittoria was a fine sculptor and a master of stucco, and his work will be found again, this time in tandem with

Fondamenta Gasparo Contarini in Canareggio: the most tranquil quarter of Venice.

that of Veronese, elsewhere in the Veneto. Sansovino will also be encountered elsewhere, less frequently but just as sensationally. As for the immense campanile itself, I find myself in agreement with the eighteenth-century English traveller and writer William Beckford (1760–1844): 'The design is barbarous and terminates in uncouth and heavy pyramids; yet in spite of these defects it struck me with awe.' When the campanile collapsed in 1902, it was rebuilt ten years later without serious alteration to the design.

The succession of state rooms in the Doge's Palace reflects not only the pomp of the by then ancient republic – for what we are seeing is essentially a rebuilding after the disastrous fires of the 1570s – but an artistic battle between Tintoretto (1518–94) and Veronese (1528–88). These two great painters of the Venetian High Renaissance are represented all over the city, and more sparsely in other parts of the Veneto, but here they are side by side. The Anticollegio contains Veronese's *Rape of Europa*, alongside paintings by Tintoretto. In the Sala del Collegio, Tintoretto has more wall space than Veronese, but it is Veronese, in his ceiling panels, who seems triumphant. These panels are vivid with Venetian colour, and display the brilliant sense of perspective which serves his equally acute sense of drama.

It is a commonplace of art history to assert that the genius of the Venetian school of painting lies in its mastery of space, light and colour, as though such mastery could be divorced from content and, on occasion, narrative. Yet the great masters were not simply finding visual counterparts to the gorgeous variety of sea and sky and light among which they lived. Titian (*c*.1487/90–1576) in the *Pesaro Madonna*, on display in the church of the Frari, was redefining the laws of composition. Veronese, here and in his other masterpieces scattered through the city, was a master of texture and knew how to capture a dramatic

---

Venice triumphant: Doge Francesco Foscari portrayed on the Doge's palace kneeling before the Lion of St Mark

moment in the midst of narrative. And even Carpaccio (*c*.1460/5–1525/6), less complex and tortured than the later painters just mentioned, was a great narrative painter, not simply a man with a genius for reflecting the richness and prettiness and flamboyance of Venice's street life.

The great chambers of the Doge's Palace were the headquarters of various ruling groups, each checking and balancing, although the real power of the republic was wielded by the Council of Ten, who, characteristically, were more than ten. By the time you reach another of these halls, the Sala del Senato, you are beginning to take for granted the opulence of gilt and stucco, the vast canvases and marble floors, and the sheer self-proclaiming, self-generating magnificence of it all. The Serenissima has imposed its own sense of grandeur and worth and historical impregnability. The irony is that all this was being done while Venice was in retreat. The celebrations of the great victory at Lepanto in 1571 were so lavish precisely because they were so badly needed in the face of Turkish advances on what had for centuries been Venice's territorial waters.

Yet there is more magnificence to come, in the Sala del Maggior Consiglio of the 1580s. Here the assembly of the Venetian nobility would meet in all its ineffectual splendour. The hall is dominated by the largest oil painting in existence, Tintoretto's *Paradise*, a far cry from Dante's medieval orderliness. If this is paradise, I'll head for other regions. Here I find myself in some sympathy with Mrs Trollope, gazing at the vast painting in about 1840: 'This seems only an elephant folio of nonsense verses, where, if there be the rhyme of art, there is none of the reason of composition . . . the whole canvas giving a feeling of violent confusion that is absolutely painful.' I prefer to direct my gaze towards the ceiling, at Veronese's painting of the apotheosis of Venice, a gloriously assembled manifestation of triumphalism, with the female figure of Venice coasting on clouds, watched from below by admiring nobles, a crowd barely controlled by horsemen, and, of course, by us. In my preference, I have Henry James on my side: 'Every one

21

here is magnificent, but the great Veronese is the most magnificent of all. . . . Never was a painter more nobly joyous, never did an artist take a greater delight in life, seeing it all as a kind of breezy festival and feeling it through the medium of perpetual success.'

After the mixture of bombast and genius, one needs, surely, a change of scale. It is time to take a look at another Venetian genius, Carpaccio, who flourished early in the sixteenth century. Walk along the Riva degli Schiavoni, the waterside promenade that runs from the Piazzetta towards the Arsenale, past the Bridge of Sighs and the luxury hotels and the gondolier stands. By the church of the Pietà, head inland and, with the help of a map and a firm sense of direction, you will come to the Scuola di San Giorgio di Schiavoni. Venice is full of these *scuole*, confraternities of the pious. Most of them are rich in painterly decoration; the best known is probably the Scuola di San Rocco, with its awesome acreage of Tintoretto. The San Giorgio di Schiavoni chapel has recently been restored, and is thus somewhat improved since Henry James's description, written in the 1880s: 'The place is small and incommodious, the pictures are out of sight and ill-lighted, the custodian is rapacious, the visitors are mutually intolerable, but the shabby little chapel is a palace of art.'

The Scuola is the preserve of Carpaccio. The confraternity was Slav in origin, yet Carpaccio's fresco cycle within seems, as do his other wonderful narrative paintings in the Accademia (this one in the Scuola is the only one still *in situ*, and all the more precious for it), quintessentially Venetian. Although some of the architectural fantasies and costumes portrayed are, to say the least, fanciful, even exotic, so was the Venice of this period, still crowded with merchants from the East. If in the Doge's Palace Tintoretto and Veronese emphasize, for obvious reasons, the pomp, the triumphalism, the power of Venice, Carpaccio seems to convey the sheer fun of the place. Where the later

---

In Venice, a figure of Noah leans against a corner of the Doge's Palace.

painters are sumptuous and sensuous, all brocades and velvets and heavy silks and powerful gestures, Carpaccio is almost dainty. His St George is no swaggering martial hero, but an almost effeminate lad, determined yet nonchalant. In the panel depicting his triumph, his admirers are gorgeously and precisely costumed, a band thumps in the background, and turbans outnumber European headwear. It's much the same in most of the succeeding panels; that depicting the exorcism is purely Venetian – the loggias and bridges, the steps of inlaid marble, the youths in multi-coloured hose. With what precision Carpaccio depicts St Augustine in his study, his books, his astrolabe, the renaissance altar, the hour-glass, the dog. If you want to know what it felt like to be a Venetian, look at Tintoretto or Veronese. If you want to know what renaissance Venice looked like, revel in Carpaccio, here and in the Accademia.

Try cutting across the back streets from the Scuola to the Arsenale. You'll probably fail, and be obliged to beg for directions, but being briefly lost in Venice is no hardship. When you reach the Arsenale, you may well feel, despite the battlements and turrets and the fearsome winged lion over the portal, that this is a slightly toytown setting for Venice's naval might. The stone menagerie by the gates only reinforces this impression: one of the lions is Greek, probably from the sixth century BC, while another, brought here as booty, was subsequently discovered to be of eleventh-century Norse origin. Yet at the height of Venice's naval and hence imperial power, this walled aquatic compound was a military machine of the utmost efficiency, using what most of us would regard as modern industrial techniques to produce warships in astonishing numbers and at astonishing speed.

The singularity of Venice means little until you have experienced the lagoon, that expanse of watery steppe which protected the city from hostile forces for century after century. The lagoon forms part of a huge estuary, itself formed by the flow of numerous Alpine rivers – the Piave, the Brenta, the Adige, and above all the Po – into the Adriatic. Sand and silt have built up into shoals and banks and, along the coast, swamps and

wetlands. Some sections of the lagoon have been preserved in all their admittedly dreary reediness, an environment that attracts a great variety of birds and other wildlife. The lagoon is filled with islands, some inhabited, most not. Between them run channels and waterways, all with their own lack of tidal predictability; this system of navigable channels was, and still is, complex, and that very complexity was the best guarantee of Venice's safety.

Boats for some of the more interesting islands in the lagoon leave from the Fondamente Nuove, a twenty-minute hike from San Marco. These boats are a good deal less frequent than most *vaporetto* services, so it is wise to consult the timetables when planning this excursion. Individual *vaporetto* journeys within Venice can become costly over the course of a few days, so it is best to avail yourself of day tickets or weekly tickets, which can be quite economical, especially when venturing out on to the lagoon. The Grand Canal is crossed at various points by inexpensive ferries called *traghetti*. These are no more than functional gondolas in which the passengers stand rather than sit so as to make the best use of the limited space. The *traghetti* compensate for the paucity of bridges across the canal and can save natives and visitors alike hours of walking each day.

The first island passed by the boat to Murano and Torcello is San Michele, a vast walled cemetery studded with pines. If being interred could be enjoyable anywhere, surely it would be here. In the far corner of the island, and best seen from the water, is the very first renaissance church in Venice, San Michele in Isola. The façade exhibits a wonderful delicacy and jewel-like exoticism made all the more fragile by its isolated setting.

The boat stops at Murano, an island famed since the thirteenth century for the quality and inventiveness of its glassware. The great majority of the products on display range from utterly tacky to kitsch to the higher

The intricate shallows of the Venetian lagoon provided the city with unique protection against invaders.

kitsch; the difference has much to do with the price tag. Other than shopping for junky glassware, the main reason for coming to Murano is to look at two churches. The larger, Santi Maria e Donato, is a Venetian-byzantine structure of great antiquity. It retains its twelfth-century campanile and a marvellous mosaic and inlay floor of 1140, mostly geometric in design but also embellished with pictures of birds. The arcades have superb capitals, though the use of terracotta gives a somewhat rude touch. In purely architectural terms, the most successful feature is the exterior of the apse, a complex galleried and balustraded structure, with rounded arches and double columns, and below the gallery lashings of zigzag ornament. Within the apse itself is a slender byzantine mosaic of the Madonna against a field of gold, and in the north aisle an impressive polychrome relief of San Donato, with tiny painted donors attributed to Paolo Veneziano (*fl.*1335–60).

The other church here is San Pietro Martire. In the south aisle is a gorgeous if over-restored Giovanni Bellini, *Madonna and Saints and the Doge Barbarigo* (1488). Bellini (1430–1516) is surely the most perfect of the Venetian painters of the early Renaissance, and the city is richly endowed with some of his loveliest works. Another painting by Bellini, the *Assumption*, used to hang here, but has been absent undergoing restoration for a very long time. Also in this aisle is a *Baptism of Christ* by Tintoretto, and opposite, in the north aisle, two fine Veroneses, notably *St Agatha in Prison*.

The boat continues across the lagoon to Torcello. Originally a Roman settlement, it was revived in the seventh century, but from the late Middle Ages fell into a gradual decline, which is now almost complete. Let John Ruskin, in a splendid passage from *The Stones of Venice* (1851–3) – still essential reading for anyone wishing to enjoy simultaneously an orgy of lush and stately prose and a passionately eccentric observation of this inimitable city – set the scene:

Seven miles to the north of Venice, the banks of sand, which near the city rise little above low-water mark,

Above **Guarded by the pure renaissance church of San Michele is the loveliest cemetery in Italy.**

Right **Venetian-byzantine architecture at its most elaborate at Santi Maria e Donato, Murano.**

attain by degrees a higher level, and knit themselves at last into fields of salt morass, raised here and there into shapeless mounds, and intercepted by narrow creeks of sea. . . . Far as the eye can reach, a waste of wild sea moor, of a lurid ashen grey; not like our northern moors with their jet-black pools and purple heath, but lifeless, the colour of sackcloth, with the corrupted sea-water soaking through the roots of its acrid weeds, and gleaming hither and thither through its snaky channels.

The tourists who come to visit Torcello's two wonderful churches will find the island scarcely altered, but for a minuscule tourist industry consisting of three restaurants, including the famous Cipriani, and a handful of souvenir stalls. Walking up the side of the canal from the jetty, the first church you reach is Santa Fosca. An early twelfth-century construction, it has a square ground plan but squinches transform the interior, which has a rounded roof. Lovely marble columns are supported on richly carved byzantine capitals. There are few furnishings of interest to obstruct the sheer architectural beauty of the church. Outside Santa Fosca is the marble hulk of the so-called Attila's throne, a seat of unknown origin, though legends abound. Other lapidary remains are strewn about this grassy piazza. Then the long brick nave of the cathedral comes into view, with its flat-roofed campanile behind.

The interior is a marvel. The marble columns and capitals resemble those of Santa Fosca, and the complex eleventh-century marble inlaid floor resembles that of Santi Maria e Donato in Murano. Hatches set into the floor permit glimpses of the even more ancient mosaic floor below. There's a ravishing pulpit and screen of slender marble columns and relief panels depicting plants and peacocks and animals, and above on the roof are fifteenth-century painted panels of the Madonna and saints. The nave extends in a sheer wall of brick from the rounded arcades up to the wooden

The stately campanile of the *duomo* watches over the sparsely inhabited island of Torcello.

roof, and this height provides the space for Torcello's greatest treasure: the byzantine mosaics at either end. The west wall depicts the Last Judgment. The saints, here and on the choir wall, have tremendous individuality, as though they were portraits of the living. In the apse is the tall elegant figure of the Madonna and Child, a thirteenth-century mosaic, and surely one of the most graceful female images in Western art. As in Murano, but to even greater effect, the Madonna shimmers against a background of nothing but gold. She entirely dominates the twelfth-century row of apostles portrayed superbly below.

It is only a short boat ride from Torcello to Burano. There is little to see here, but the terraces of houses along the canals, painted vivid blue or lilac or green, have a charm rarely found in Veneto villages. Small boats are moored along the quays, some of them makeshift shops. In the church of San Martino is a typically flamboyant *Crucifixion* (1725) by G. B. Tiepolo (1696–1770) whose domestic frescoes in the villas of the Veneto are often more successful than his supposedly religious works. Beside the church is the Piazza Galuppi and the main street of the same name, lined with cafés and fish restaurants. In the piazza is the Scuola dei Merletti, the lacemaking museum. Most of the lace seen for sale on the island is of foreign manufacture, and best avoided. Another island, much closer to Venice and facing the Doge's Palace, is dominated by a major church by Palladio, the great innovative architect of the Veneto. His work dominates Vicenza and much of the surrounding countryside, yet his commissions in Venice were few, and most of them were for churches rather than for the villas with which he made his reputation. The commission of 1565 to rebuild the island monastery of San Giorgio Maggiore was of colossal importance if only because the site was so spectacular. Thus the boat ride out to San Giorgio is delectable not only because it grants access to the great church but because of the lovely view back towards the Palace and San Marco. Henry James, writing in 1883 in *Portraits of Places*, had mixed feelings about San Giorgio, 'which, for an ugly Palladian church, has a success beyond all reason. It

Right **A masterpiece of byzantine art: the mosaic Madonna and Child at Torcello.**

Far right **The grandest of Palladio's churches in Venice: San Giorgio Maggiore.**

is a success of position, of colour, of the immense detached Campanile.'

Palladio's church, one of the major landmarks – and seamarks – of Venice, has tremendous authority, and is conceived, like all his major designs, as a unified and impeccably proportioned whole. The double façade is one of his hallmarks, and the interior has redoubtable confidence. The pilasters and columns of the interior echo those of the façade (strictly, the other way round, as the façade was completed after Palladio's death in 1580, but to his design). The nave is a stately progression of grey and white, complex but logical, magisterial but, it has to be said, cold. Any warmth the church possesses derives from the richly carved choir stalls, separated from the church by an open screen of fluted columns, and the discreet presence of three late paintings by Tintoretto, on a grand scale yet far more accessible than the indigestible performances in the Doge's Palace. I also like the view back from the crossing on to niches and cornices and statues, giving a note of theatricality otherwise missing from this wonderful but austere church. San Giorgio's baleful influence is seen all over the Veneto, indeed Italy, in a succession of correct but often dreary neo-classical churches built to a coarser version of Palladio's motifs, right up to the end of the last century.

Take another *vaporetto* over to the Giudecca, getting off at Redentore. You'll pass the disappointing façade of the Zitelle church, partly by Palladio, which is compensated for by the wonderful façade of the Redentore. Like that of San Giorgio, it looks better from afar, when the interplay of marble and dome and statue is fully realized. The Redentore façade is more compact if less authoritative than that of San Giorgio, and Palladio's favourite pediment motif is used no fewer than four times. Palladio did not simply adopt the standard forms of classical architecture; his genius lay in part in his ability to use and reuse them in daring combinations, without ever jeopardizing the essential

The ornamented prow of a gondola bobs amid the mooring poles of the Molo.

harmoniousness of the design. Palladio's designs are never pastiche, but original reworkings of the standard motifs of classical forms.

From afar one can see the dome and the statue of Christ the Redeemer, a reminder that the church was begun in 1577 to give thanks for the ending of a disastrous plague. The church is approached up a flight of steps reminiscent of the entrances to some of Palladio's villas. Where San Giorgio has a domed crossing, here the balustraded dome is over the high altar. In San Giorgio the screen between altar and monks' choir is straight, but here it is curved back, rounding out the design. The interior has greater warmth, even intimacy, than San Giorgio but not at the expense of grandeur and intense seriousness.

Across the Giudecca Canal from the Redentore is the broad promenade known as the Zattere. Lined with ice-cream parlours, pizzerias and bars, it's a good place to unwind, and is far less crowded than the cafés around San Marco. While sipping *prosecco*, the excellent sparkling wine of the Veneto, or lapping an ice, one can watch the ferries and cruise liners slide up the Giudecca Canal, and in the late afternoon the setting sun lights up the dome of the Redentore. Schooners sometimes moor here, and the waters are usually thick with *vaporetti*. Walk up the side of one of the canals that breaks the line of the Zattere, the Rio San Trovaso, and you will soon come to one of the more curious sights of Venice: the Squero. This is the repair shop for disabled gondolas, yet it seems curiously out of place, since the yard is surrounded by wooden huts with wooden balconies, more reminiscent of an Alpine village than a Venetian backwater. A few yards away, near the church of San Trovaso, stands a tree. I remark upon this because greenery is something of a rarity in Venice. In the eighteenth century, Arthur Young, a seasoned traveller, was remarking with dismay about Venice: 'Not a field nor a bush even for fancy to pluck a rose from!'

It's a short walk from here to the great art galleries of the Accademia, and by remaining on the same side of the Grand Canal as the Accademia, one soon comes to the church of Santa Maria della Salute (1630). This

is the work of Longhena (1598–1682) and, like the Redentore, was commissioned to give thanks for the ending of a bout of plague. The Salute may not be the loveliest church in Venice, nor the most fascinating, nor the most spiritual, yet I suspect it is my favourite, for it is so quintessentially Venetian, with those theatrical scrolls around the dome, the dozens of statues posing like crazy, the byzantine and Palladian references of the domes, and the Palladian homage of the semicircular mullioned windows (known as thermal or Diocletian windows) and the grey-and-white interior colouring reminiscent of San Giorgio.

The sacristy contains, among other great paintings, one of Tintoretto's most masterly works, his *Marriage at Cana* (1561). John Ruskin found brilliance of design and signs of the highest genius even in Tintoretto's sardine-can vision of Paradise in the Doge's Palace, and the large painting here in the Salute excited him still more:

> The picture is perhaps the most perfect example which human art has produced of the utmost possible force and sharpness of shadow united with richness of local colour. This picture unites colour as rich as Titian's with light and shade as forcible as Rembrandt's, and far more decisive.

Such is the richness of the essentially octagonal design of the Salute that the church looks good, and different, from all angles, but one of the best views is from the *traghetto* stop alongside the Gritti Palace on the other side of the Grand Canal. From here one can also see, to the right, the equally Venetian Ca' Dario of 1487 alongside the canal, with its lopsided windows and the lovely inlaid marble roundels on the façade and its medieval chimneys. (Many Venetian palaces are called Ca' rather than Palazzo.)

Ca' Dario always puts me in mind of an even lovelier example of the same style of architecture, the church of

---

Santa Maria della Salute, at the spot where the Grand Canal meets the lagoon.

Santa Maria dei Miracoli just north of the Rialto Bridge. Dating from the 1480s, it is the work of the Lombardo family, whose ravishing craftsmanship adds grace and beauty to many major buildings of the Veneto. Some of their other designs equal that of Miracoli; none surpasses it. It is essentially the conception of Pietro Lombardo (1435–1515), with embellishments by his son Tullio. Set right alongside a canal, it seems to float like a small galleon. Its panels of coloured marble and its sheer shapeliness – reminiscent of the slightly earlier church on the island of San Michele – show a passionate delight in all the resources of renaissance decoration: the fluted pilasters, the window mouldings, the gracious curved gables, the roundels of inlaid marble and porphyry, the friezes and medallions.

Perhaps one could level the charge of preciosity against this casket-like church, but I shan't. Moreover, the interior is utterly bewitching, surprisingly capacious, and grandly sheltered beneath a coffered and painted wooden roof. The walls are relatively restrained in their use of decorative devices, but not the choir, which is raised and lined with pulpits and balustrades with half-figures by Tullio on either side of the steps. Soaring above the choir is the cupola. Within the choir is more inlay work: Tullio's openwork marble altar, and a riot of ornament at the base of the choir arch. Despite this lavishness, the overall impression is of restraint and elegance; the architectural form, directing the eye up to the miraculous image of the Madonna on the altar, is, finally, more important than the ornament. Nothing could be more remote from the baroque, which incessantly calls attention to its own virtuosity.

From a single gem to a tiara. Across the Grand Canal, in the San Polo quarter, is the immense Franciscan church of the Frari. This vast gothic edifice, with its massive piers, its cross-beams and ribs, has become a depository for the post-mortem reputation of great Venetians. The walls are packed with monuments that reach to the roof, with altars and tombs filling the remaining space. The monument to Canova (1757–1822) is just one of a number of indications in the Veneto that the great sculptor had considerable

ego, though it is only fair to mention that the monument was originally intended to commemorate Titian, not its designer. To explore the Frari takes half a day, so I will point to just a few of its contents.

This is perhaps the best spot in Venice to make the acquaintance of Titian, for the Frari contains two of his masterpieces. In the north aisle his *Pesaro Madonna* is rich in resplendent colour. The composition is daring too, for the Madonna is almost upstaged by the kneeling Pesaro family, with St Peter, gorgeous in blue and yellow, as stage manager. The worldly encroaches on the religious, and almost has the edge. The art historian E. H. Gombrich has explained both the shock and the success of the painting: 'Titian's contemporaries may well have been amazed at the audacity with which he had dared to upset the old-established rules of composition. They must have expected, at first, to find such a picture lopsided and unbalanced. Actually it is the opposite.'

An even more luscious and stunning painting fills the choir: his intensely dramatic *Assumption*, in which the Virgin is propelled upwards to the acclaim of angels, her arms outstretched in ecstatic anticipation. In a south choir chapel is a wonderful statue of an emaciated John the Baptist by Donatello (1386–1466), a Florentine sculptor, but one whose work, always of the very highest quality, is found in generous quantities in the Veneto.

In the south transept chapel is a magical *Madonna and Saints* by Giovanni Bellini, a work of the most ravishing beauty, utterly flawless. Henry James got it right when he wrote of it over a century ago:

Nothing in Venice is more perfect than this, and we know of no work of art more complete . . . It is impossible to imagine anything more finished or more

ripe. It is one of those things that sum up the genius of a painter, the experience of a life, the teaching of a school.

On one occasion when I visited the Frari this part of the church was blocked off because a wedding was taking place, and I waited an hour to dart in after the interminable ceremony. A sacristan, anxious to close the church, was soon after me, but I snatched one minute in front of this perfect painting before being evicted, and the sixty-minute wait seemed a small price to pay.

Such delays and distractions must be met with good humour, for they are unavoidable in Italy. The best laid plans and itineraries are invariably sabotaged by the irregularity of opening hours – some churches close at noon, others at twelve-thirty; some reopen at three, some at four, some the next morning – and by the Italian passion for interminable restoration schemes. Some of the most fascinating sights in all the Veneto – the anatomical theatre in Padua is but one example – are *in restauro*, and if you inquire when the restoration is due to be completed, the answer is almost always a shrug. Sometimes *in restauro* is a euphemism for staff shortages, but whatever the reason it is maddening to make a special journey only to be greeted with locks and a fading sign. In the major cities it is essential to check with the local tourist office, which should have a list of churches and museums and *palazzi*, giving opening hours and specifying which monuments are temporarily closed.

These and other frustrations fade into insignificance after a while, for the Veneto is rich in culture and beauty and variety. It is also well endowed with those other essential ingredients of satisfactory travelling, excellent cuisine and invigorating wines. In the chapters that follow we shall encounter them all.

The most perfect renaissance church in Venice: Santa Maria dei Miracoli.

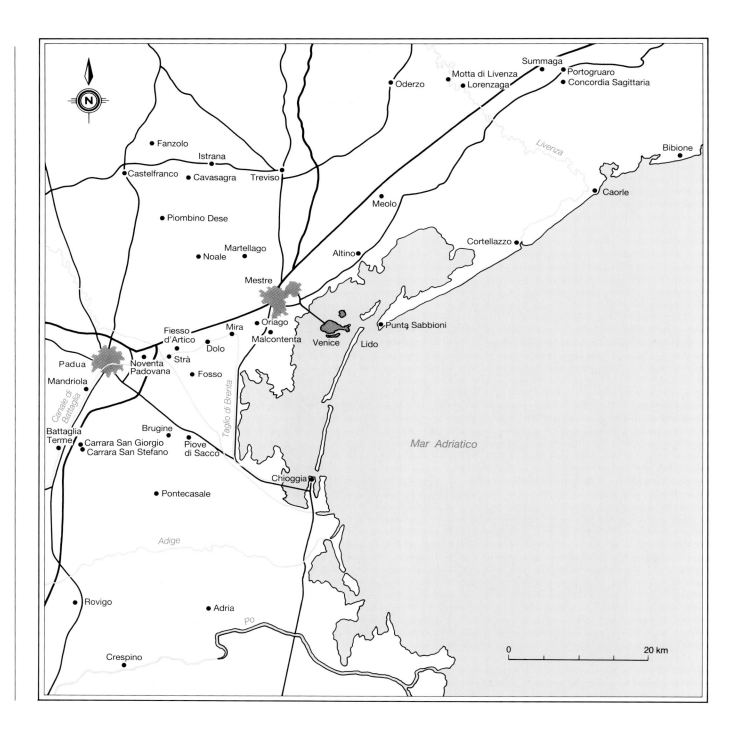

Fanzolo
Istrana
Castelfranco   Cavasagra   Treviso
Piombino Dese
Martellago
Noale
Mestre
Fiesso   Mira   Oriago
d'Artico   Malcontenta
Dolo   Venice   Lido
Padua   Strà
Noventa   Fosso
Padovana
Mandriola
Battaglia
Terme   Brugine
Carrara San Giorgio   Piove
Carrara San Stefano   di Sacco
Canale di Battaglia
Taglio di Brenta
Chioggia
Pontecasale
Adige
Rovigo   Adria
Po
Crespino

Oderzo
Summaga
Motta di Livenza   Portogruaro
Lorenzaga   Concordia Sagittaria
Livenza   Bibione
Meolo   Caorle
Cortellazzo
Altino
Punta Sabbioni
Mar Adriatico

0   20 km

1
Around the Lagoon

Portogruaro – Treviso – Castelfranco – the Brenta Canal –
Rovigo – Chioggia

Since Venice itself is a city where the distinction between water and land sometimes becomes blurred, most notoriously during times of flood, it is scarcely surprising that the area around the city is flat and topographically uneventful. Both north-east and south-west of Venice, near the delta of the River Po, the landscape is almost entirely flat, a monotony of fields divided by canals and dykes. Although unarguably monotonous, it is not necessarily dreary, and there are times of the day and of the year when this immense bleak landscape beneath vast skies acquires an oddly magical quality.

This quality is, however, absent from the coastal strips just east and north of the city. An ample supply of sandy beaches has led to the development of these strips as beach resorts. Venice's Lido, a short ferry ride from the outskirts of the city, is among the oldest and most celebrated, and the grand old hotels have an antique majesty of a kind. The great majority of visitors, however, must find quarters in the more modern and anonymous hotels that line the beaches, and the streets parallel to the beaches, for several kilometres. It is only a brief crossing from the northern tip of the Lido to Punta Sabbioni on the spit of the mainland. From Punta Sabbioni to Cortellazzo, a stretch of some 24 kilometres, the hotels are ranged two or three deep along the shore.

The southern part of the spit can be traversed by an inland road which takes you along the side of the lagoon. This too is a dispiriting journey, for it offers the prospect of rubbish-strewn, reedy islets, jetties, houses and light industrial depots. The thirty kilometres of inletted shore beyond Cortellazzo to the border of the Veneto with Friuli has also been thoroughly exploited by the beach resort industry. Bibione, the most northerly, is crisp and modern, but characterless. Caorle, on the other hand, does have some personality of its own, for it is a real town, with an ancient church and narrow lanes, as well as the seemingly endless string of hotels along the excellent beaches on either side of the port. The basilica dates from the eleventh century, and has a warm and spacious interior with alternating brick and marble piers. The brick campanile not only leans, but is round, with a conical roof. And the landscape by the edge of the lagoon at the far eastern end of town is of some interest. Fishing boats are moored at the jetties, and sea birds scream from their nests on the far shore. Here at last is a touch of wildness.

From Caorle head north and inland towards Portogruaro. Even away from the coast the landscape remains utterly flat. Tractors toil over thick clay fields unrelieved by trees and hedgerows, and the only breaks other than roads are the many rivers that flow

Above At Caorle, a campanile on the very edge of the Adriatic.

Right Near Lanzoni, the shallow but sometimes treacherous waters of the Venetian lagoon.

into the Adriatic. Most of them are lined initially with lofty reeds and then by dykes. You can drive along the top of the dykes that flank the River Livenza, and this gives you the best views of a landscape in which there are no views. Here and there you see huge nets suspended over the rivers and canals – fishing the easy way. Only the solid brick farmhouses, usually of three storeys with barns attached, and distant campaniles show that the area is inhabited. Living and farming here can be a risky matter; many churches have plaques that record alarming flood levels. At Motta di Livenza, to the north-west, the waters reached a level of almost 2.5 metres in 1966, flooding the entire town.

Just before Portogruaro you will come to Concordia Sagittaria, a small town of Roman origin founded in the first century BC by Julius Caesar and built along the banks of a river. The originally romanesque basilica was virtually rebuilt in 1466, but the late twelfth-century campanile remains unaltered, as does the even earlier baptistery. The interior of the basilica is a disappointment, despite the beautifully carved font. The little eleventh-century baptistery, built in the shape of a Greek cross, shows byzantine influence; it also contains early medieval frescoes. Lapidary remains are embedded in the façade of a small building behind the baptistery. All around the church are excavations: early Christian tombs and a fourth-century church have been uncovered near the basilica, and a kilometre away, along the Venice road, are the remains of a Roman bridge of the second century.

Portogruaro has been unfairly dismissed by writer and architectural historian John Julius Norwich as 'a sad and featureless town', and he notes that when the Venetian general Nicolò Canal was found guilty in 1470 of various military failures, banishment to Portogruaro was deemed punishment enough. Before it joined the Venetian lands in 1420, the area was ruled by the patriarchs of Aquileia. Portogruaro won special trading privileges from Venice in return for services rendered, and this accounts for its relative wealth during the renaissance period. The old town lies just north of the main Trieste–Venice road. Follow Borgo San Giovanni towards the old quarter. The small church of San Giovanni on the right has frescoes of varying quality and a very pretty painted wooden roof. You enter the old city proper across a bridge – one of many, for the town is criss-crossed by rivers and canals, not unlike Venice itself – and pass beneath the San Giovanni gate (originally gothic but rebuilt in 1555). The Borgo now changes its name to Corso Martiri, which is lined with skinny palm trees in the middle and arcaded houses, many old, on either side. A pillar with the winged lion of Venice is a reminder of the town's allegiance. The Corso does a slow curve into Piazza della Repubblica, where stands the Palazzo Comunale, a modest, much restored building, with stepped castellations alluding to its gothic origin. Next to the *palazzo* is a charming renaissance fountain: two bronze cranes replenish the marble bowl through their beaks.

Behind the *palazzo* a piazzetta overlooks the weir of the principal river, the Lemene. On the opposite bank waterfowl trot on the grass; behind them walls enclose the gardens of old houses along Via del Seminario. To the right, beneath the arcades of a fifteenth-century house, is a delightful wooden fishermen's oratory of 1627. Return to the main street, and walk past the leaning romanesque campanile and the dull eighteenth-century *duomo* (though with an attractive fourteenth-century relief of the Madonna on the exterior of the apse). Continue along the Corso, where there are some splendid fifteenth-century *palazzi* on the left.

Take the lane alongside the *duomo*, cross to the other side of the river, and turn right. You are at the spot where Via del Seminario changes its name to Via Garibaldi, both streets studded with attractive renaissance arcaded houses. You are also standing next to the Antico Spessotto, the best hotel and most elegant restaurant in town. No. 22 Via del Seminario is the Museo Concordiese, where Roman capitals, statues, mosaics and inscriptions from Concordia Sagittaria are displayed in the main hall. Just inside the museum entrance is a very fine early medieval relief of the seated Madonna and Child, which retains much of the its original paintwork. Most of the houses and *palazzi* in Via del Seminario have been thoroughly restored, as

Arcades offer shelter along the main streets of Portogruaro.

have those in its continuation, Via Cavour. But no. 1 is a commanding example of a fifteenth-century *palazzo* with renaissance ornament overlaying a gothic structure. At the end of Via Cavour you leave the old city through a tower of gothic origin and return to the main road.

As a site of historical importance, Summaga, just west of Portogruaro, can't rival Concordia, but the early thirteenth-century church here is much more satisfying. Its simple romanesque lines are marred only by the neo-classical west façade, though the fine campanile is intact. So is the lovely interior, all of mellow brick and adorned on walls, piers, and apse with frescoes. Those in the apse – the Madonna enthroned and below her a row of apostles and other scenes – are early thirteenth-century and especially fine. Only fragments of the precious eleventh-century frescoes remain in the adjoining absidal chapel – presumably part of an earlier structure – but these include a Crucifixion and some striking secular images, such as a griffin.

Although this region to the north of the Venetian lagoon isn't packed with interest, a few of the towns here are worth a quick visit. About 30 km west of Portogruaro, Motta di Livenza boasts two substantial churches. In the centre of town is the sixteenth-century *duomo*, which contains among the altar-pieces a post-Veronese painting by Leandro Bassano (1558–1623). The other church is the Santuario della Madonna dei Miracoli (1513). The sides of the basilica are pleasantly arcaded, and the curved façade is embellished with statues. The focal point of the basilica is the crypt-like chapel at the east end of the north aisle. Before descending into the crypt, pause to look at Palma Giovane's *Assumption*, the best of the sixteenth-century paintings in the church. The crypt marks the spot where the Madonna appeared on 9 March 1510 to Giovanni Cigana; a transcription of her message is on the walls. The marble relief over the high altar is late sixteenth-century and exploits perspective to pleasingly elegant effect. The basilica's supplicatory mood is broken by the aviary in the cloister.

At Lorenzaga, just south of Motta on the road to Caorle, the church has a stylish neo-classical interior and lavishly carved choir stalls. But Oderzo, a few kilometres west of Motta, is more worthwhile. The town dates back to the Roman era, although artefacts from those times are visible only in the municipal museum. In the main square, Piazza Vittorio Emanuele, a few arcaded sixteenth-century houses adjoin a far grander early-renaissance group, the Loggia Pretoria. A brick gateway leads to another pleasant arcaded group in the Piazza Pompeo Tomitano. The *duomo*, with its excessively tall campanile, dates from the thirteenth century but has been heavily restored and enlarged subsequently. The west façade, usually the most lavish face of any church, is here eclipsed by the gothic south portal, which is also frescoed. The interior is barnlike, but worth visiting to see the medieval frescoes, albeit damaged, on the nave walls. Most towns in the Veneto can boast a native artist, and Oderzo is no exception, but the paintings on the south

wall by Pomponio Amalteo (1505–88) are gloomily conventional. In the east chapel of the south aisle is a fifteenth-century *Madonna* by Andrea Bellunello (1430–94).

South of Oderzo, in Méolo, the church has sketchy, mostly monochrome frescoes by G. B. Tiepolo (1758) above the choir, and a vivid baroque altar-piece. Of considerably more interest is a cluster of buildings a few kilometres further south. This is Altino, the former Roman town of Altinum, which Attila destroyed in 452. Since the seventh century Altino has been uninhabited, and the hamlet's principal building is the museum, where archaeological finds from the digs still being conducted around the building are on display. In the field opposite the museum you can see mosaic pavements left *in situ*.

The almost ghostly calm of Altino is in strong contrast to the bustling self-confidence of nearby Treviso, one of the most enjoyable towns of the Veneto. Of Bronze Age origin, Treviso was of considerable importance in Roman times, though it suffered the usual devastation following the Barbarian invasions. It recovered sufficiently to become a major cultural centre in the thirteenth century, only to succumb to a succession of warlords. It is slightly ironic that after this rich history, Treviso should now be most celebrated for the lettuce known as radicchio, a very tasty and versatile product that is eaten cooked in innumerable ways as well as in salads. Another local speciality is a rich soup called *sopa coada* made from chicken or pigeon or other fowl stewed among layers of bread. With far more to offer than gastronomy, Treviso remains one of the least appreciated cities of the Veneto. There is nothing touristy about it, even though it is packed with buildings of great interest. Moreover, the town itself, with its canals and painted houses and fortifications, has considerable charm and is easily negotiable on foot.

The Venetians prudently renewed the town fortifications, and it is worth making a circuit of the town to

The fishermen's oratory at Portogruaro.

see the largely intact early sixteenth-century walls. On the north side, near the Belluno road, is the finest of the gates, Porta San Tommaso, a chunky mass of white stone, built by Giuglielmo Bergamasco (1518). Entering Treviso from the west you pass through Porta dei Santi Quaranta, a stylish renaissance gateway of 1517, with pilasters framing a winged lion in the centre.

Make for the centrally situated *duomo*. Its heavy nineteenth-century portico is flanked by two stone creatures left over from a previous romanesque cathedral, though to me they resemble rejected Muppets. The interior is much more satisfactory, with its series of domes over the nave and its barrel-vaulted aisles. In the south aisle, against two piers, are fine sculptures: a bas-relief by Lorenzo Bregno, and Vittoria's operatic *John the Baptist*. In the south choir chapel are an *Annunciation* by Titian and striking frescoes of the Adoration of the Magi by Pordenone (1483–1539). The chapel also contains the sophisticated tomb of Bishop Castellano (1332), two fine paintings by Paris Bordone (1500–71), and a *Madonna and Saints* by Girolamo da Treviso. In the north choir chapel is the beautifully framed renaissance tomb of Bishop Franco (1501) and, in the domed apse of the chapel, stylish statues by Lorenzo Bregno, executed between 1509 and 1513. In the choir itself, behind the altar, is a resplendent early sixteenth-century sarcophagus panelled with half-figures in relief. On the north wall is Pietro Lombardo's tomb of Bishop Zanetto (1485). The crypt dates from the ninth century, but has long been inaccessible because of restoration work.

To the north of the *duomo* is the stout brick campanile, to which is attached the thirteenth-century baptistery. Between the baptistery and the cathedral is the narrow entry into the Vicolo del Duomo, which gives access to the medieval canons' houses and the cathedral archives. Emerge into Via Bordone, with its gothic towers. Turn left, then right into Calmaggiore, which brings you into Piazza dei Signori. The building facing you is the battlemented and restored Palazzo dei Trecento, the early thirteenth-century town hall where the 150 nobles and 150 citizens of Treviso would meet in council. Below the great hall, rebuilt

after bomb damage during World War II, is a large arcaded loggia, now an outdoor café. Adjoining the Palazzo is the Prefettura, a nineteenth-century reconstruction, and behind it a tall battlemented tower.

Take the passage between the two *palazzi*, accurately named the Soffioni ('draughty passage'), which brings you to the courtyard of the Monte di Pietà. (A *monte di pietà* is a pawnbroker's. I do not know why such establishments in Italy are built on so large a scale, but they seem to have combined charitable functions with commercial ones.) In the left corner a passage leads to the pretty and atmospheric fourteenth-century church of Santa Lucia. The south aisle and chapel retain fragmentary frescoes by pupils of Tomaso da Modena (1323–79), notably a fine vernacular Crucifixion. One of the delights of visiting Treviso is the opportunity to discover and relish the work of this splendid mid fourteenth-century painter, whose frescoes are concentrated in the city's churches. Around the choir are late-gothic bas reliefs, and a charmingly carved altar rail with half-figures – all of fine quality. To the south of Santa Lucia is the church of San Vito – they share a common wall. This is a less attractive renaissance building, but has interesting contents, including an altar-piece by Marco Vecellio (1545–1611) in the choir, and beside it a gothic tabernacle of 1363 of more than usual complexity. Badly faded frescoes in the south apse, only uncovered in 1926, are byzantine in style but hard to make out.

On leaving the churches turn right at the fountain down Via Campana and you'll soon reach Ponte Buranelli, one of many little bridges crossing Treviso's canals. The view from here is especially charming. Continue across another larger bridge and you'll come to the narrow-aisled church of San Francesco. Long disused, it was restored in the 1920s. The nave is covered with a spectacular keel roof. San Francesco has acquired fame by association, as the south aisle contains a monument to Petrarch's daughter Francesca (1384) and the north transept is the final resting place

In Treviso, as in every town of the Veneto, an inventive fountain gushes.

of Dante's son Pietro Alighieri, who died here in 1364. Tomaso da Modena and his pupils painted most of the frescoes in the choir chapels, notably the enthroned Madonna in the north chapel.

Continue past the rear of the church along a street which contains some of the painted façades – often with a pink diaper pattern – for which Treviso is famous. Turn right down Via Manzoni; you will pass the oval church of San Agostino, with its prettily stuccoed interior and fifteenth-century frescoes (brought here from another church) and carved Crucifix in the style of Andrea Brustolon (1662–1732), the Veneto's major sculptor of the early eighteenth century. Keep going straight to the curiously curved gothic façade of Santa Maria Maggiore. The nave is gothic, but not the transepts and choir, which are in a Lombard renaissance style. The north transept houses a revered image of the Madonna, painted enthroned by Tomaso da Modena. In front of it stands an elegant

The city walls of Treviso now frame a verdant park.

colonnaded chapel with inlaid marble. Adjoining the transept is a semicircular domed baptistery, with mid sixteenth-century frescoes.

With the church behind you, walk down Via Carlo Alberto, past some remarkable old arcaded houses. Turn left down Via San Leonardo to the church of that name, crossing another bridge and passing a mill-wheel on the right. In a south chapel of the church is a small, finely detailed triptych from the workshop of Cima da Conegliano. On leaving the church turn right, then left down Via San Agostino, bearing left after the church down Vicolo Pescheria, with its gothic houses. You'll now be at the fish market, located since medieval times on an islet in the river. Cross the bridge and continue towards Piazza dei Signori. On the left down Via Palestro is the restored Casa dei Carraresi. Turn left down Via San Michele, just before the piazza, and you'll find on the right the thirteenth-century Loggia dei Cavalieri, where the nobles and gallants of Treviso used to entertain themselves. War damage ruined the frescoes for which the loggia was celebrated. Walk past the loggia down Via Martiri della Libertà, turn right down Via Diaz and you will reach the vast brick church of San Nicolò, with its superb polygonal apses and lofty campanile.

The interior is equally splendid, with its arcades over tall rounded piers, and a slender intricate keel roof that runs the length of the very long nave. Such are the dimensions of the church that even the most grotesque baroque altars fade into insignificance. The most unusual feature of San Nicolò is the frescoing of some of the piers. Just by the north door are some admirably vivid and characterful frescoes by Tomaso da Modena, notably St Jerome and St Agnes. Many of the other pier frescoes are by Tomaso's pupils and they too are of good quality. Opposite the north door is a beautiful sixteenth-century altar-piece, carved with renaissance confidence by Lorenzo Bregno. Also in the south aisle is a colossal and quite absurd fresco of St

Christopher (1410) by Antonio da Treviso. The high altar and altar rails are good lively baroque work. On the north side of the choir is the magnificent tomb of Agostino d'Onigo (c.1500), whose dignified statue stands on the lid; the tomb, probably from the Lombardo workshop, is framed within a decorative renaissance fresco. In the south transept are an early fifteenth-century polychrome *Pietà* and rather poor frescoes, but the south-east choir chapels have early fourteenth-century frescoes of notable quality. The chapel between this one and the choir has Sienese frescoes and an altar-piece attributed to Lorenzo Lotto (1480–1556), but has been closed for restoration.

A door in the south aisle leads to the sumptuously panelled sacristy with its coffered ceiling. But the remaining treasure of this church must be reached through the seminary alongside the west front. Off the cloister is a remarkable chapter-house, painted on three sides with portraits of monks by Tomaso da Modena in 1352. It also contains a poignant though damaged fresco of the Crucifixion in byzantine style.

With the north door of San Nicolò behind you, take the street opposite back to the *duomo*. From Piazza del Duomo, it's a short walk to the Museo Civico along the road opposite the cathedral portico, Via Riccati, then left down Borgo Cavour. The museum contains an extensive collection of paintings by almost all the principal artists of the Veneto, from frescoes by medieval masters such as Tomaso da Modena to works by Giovanni Bellini, Cima da Conegliano (c.1459–c.1517), Lotto, Titian, Jacopo Bassano, Pietro Longhi, and the Tiepolos. Bassano's *Crucifixion*, in its depiction of light and cloud, was to have a considerable influence on, not surprisingly, El Greco.

On leaving Treviso take the Vicenza road. You will pass through Istrana, where there is a fine villa on the left. Just before Castelfranco, bear right to Fanzolo, where on the edge of the village is Palladio's magisterial Villa Emo (1564). A shallow ramp leads up to a deep pedimented portico on Doric columns. There is one bay on either side of the portico, and then the usual barchesses (colonnades sheltering wings used for agricultural purposes). The interior is frescoed by

Not Venice, but Treviso, another city crisscrossed by canals.

Giovanni Battista Zelotti (1526–78). The villa is in complete harmony with its surroundings; garden paths, steps and arcades, all have their designated place and proportion around this airy house, which, unusually for a Veneto villa, was lived in by the same family for centuries.

South-east of Fanzolo, across the main road, is Cavasagra, where stands the splendid, porticoed, mid eighteenth-century Villa Corner, now a hotel and restaurant set within a lovely park. The *piano nobile* has been converted into suites of vast height and size.

Continue west to Castelfranco, a splendid walled and moated town, more characterful than its nearby rival Cittadella. The grassy area and fosse outside the walls have been beautifully planted to form the town's public gardens, and there are cafés and shops all around the walls on the other side of the boulevard. It's a small town and thus a quick walk to the *duomo*, marked by a medieval campanile and set behind a pleasant balustraded forecourt; to the right is a renaissance *palazzo*, now used as a library. The *duomo* itself contains, off the south transept, one of the Veneto's great treasures, Giorgione's sumptuous and wonderfully poised *Madonna and Saints*. It was commissioned by one Tuzio Costanzo in memory of his son Matteo, who had died in 1504. The commission was wonderfully fulfilled. Castelfranco was Giorgione's birthplace, and alongside the church at no. 15 Vicolo della Chiesa is the modest house where he is supposed to have been born in 1477 or 1478. Giorgione, about whom very little is known, is one of the most mysterious of the renaissance masters, and only about twenty of his works survive. He was undoubtedly influenced by the great Venetian masters who preceded him, such as Giovanni Bellini, but there are signs in his work that he had also studied the work of north European artists such as Albrecht Dürer (1471–1528).

The American art critic Bernard Berenson (1865–1959) wrote:

> Giorgione combined the fine feeling and poetry of Bellini with Carpaccio's gaiety and love of beauty and colour. . . . Giorgione painted pictures so perfectly in touch with the ripened spirit of the Renaissance that they met with the success which those things only find that at the same moment wake us to the full sense of a need and satisfy it.

That attempt to place Giorgione strikes me as a trifle over-expansive, even mystical. The difficulty, it seems to me, is that it is hard to see Giorgione's work, slender though his corpus is, as a coherent unity. His most famous and daring composition, called *The Tempest* and to this day unelucidated by art historians, may be seen in the Accademia in Venice. Rich and mysterious it undoubtedly is, yet it seems very different in texture, mood and composition from the marvellous, poised and virtually flawless altar-piece here in Castelfranco. Many of his extant works are fragmentary, which makes the survival of this splendid painting all the more gratifying. It is also one of the few works attributed to Giorgione that no scholar disputes.

When leaving Castelfranco, head south-east to Piombino Dese. In the town centre stands Palladio's Villa Cornaro, begun in 1553 but not completed till 1596, sixteen years after his death. With its two-storey projecting loggia and pediment, it's a striking and handsome composition. The outer bays are lower but symmetrical. The pediment focuses round a star in an open circle, another original element in the design.

Continue south-east to Noale. Along the main road is a stylishly arcaded loggia, and a few yards away a splendid fortified medieval gateway of the former thirteenth-century castle leads into the piazza with its delightful arcaded houses. At the far end of the square is another fortified gate with a lofty battlemented belfry. Pass through this gate and on the right you'll see the small oratory that apparently contains fifteenth-century marble altars. Other remains of the castle walls and towers now enclose the cemetery a short distance to the south. If you're feeling hungry, the village of Stigliano not far south of Noale boasts another battlemented castle which is now a restaurant.

Dawn casts the sun's rays beneath a medieval gateway at Castelfranco.

East of Noale is Martellago, where you'll find the square-cut sixteenth-century Villa Grimani-Morosino. Its façade has frescoes by Zelotti, and there are energetic eighteenth-century statues over the various gates. A few kilometres further and you are in Mestre, the huge industrial and suburban sprawl on the mainland side of the Venice causeway. Having spent twenty minutes driving around central Mestre without realizing I was there, I advise you to give this amorphous urban mass a miss. The few buildings of interest hardly justify the torments of the *tangenziale*, two dozen roundabouts, and the one-way system of the town centre. Instead take the Ravenna road, and bear left into Malcontenta.

On the left by the Brenta canal bridge is the awesome Villa Foscari by Palladio (1560). It is awesome not because of its size, though the *piano nobile* is splendidly lofty, but because of its compact power, equally characteristic of the Tempietto at Maser. Over the portico pediment is a second attic pediment – once again, an original treatment by Palladio of this architectural theme. The tall chimneys rising from the shallow roof add to the strongly vertical thrust of the portico. Another unconventional feature is the placing of the steps to the *piano nobile* on the outer bays, thus converting the portico into a kind of loggia. The interior is frescoed with mythological scenes by the ubiquitous Zelotti.

Head north-west out of Malcontenta, and follow signs for Padua. You will soon be at Oriago, the first stopping place along the crowded Brenta canal that runs from Mestre to Padua, with villas every step of the way. There are over two thousand villas in the Veneto, many of them concentrated along this stretch of waterway and its subsidiary canals, which was developed as a kind of resort for rich Venetians as early as the late fifteenth century and blossomed throughout the following century. Whatever the guidebooks say, it is in practice extremely difficult to find some of the

The mighty walls that surround Castelfranco.

The romanticized statue of the painter Giorgione at his birthplace, Castelfranco.

more important villas and equally difficult to identify them once you have found them. Most of them are not open to visitors, and can only be glimpsed, if at all, through gates or down an avenue of trees. To point out and inspect each villa of interest – and in many cases the interest lies in their inaccessible frescoes – would be almost impossible, so it is probably best to drive as slowly as the incessant traffic in this very built-up area permits and to pause when a building grabs your attention. The most painless way to visit the Brenta canal is by the luxurious motorboat known as *Il Burchiello*, which plies the route between Venice and Padua during the summer months, pausing at some of the more celebrated villas en route.

During the eighteenth and nineteenth centuries many of the villas were allowed to deteriorate, and the Brenta canal presented a less luxurious aspect than it does today. James Fennimore Cooper, writing his *Excursions in Italy* in the 1830s and showing himself not the most discerning of travellers in Europe, remarked with New World condescension: 'The houses themselves were well enough; but the monotony of a country as level as Holland, and the landscape gardening that is confined to flowers and allées and exotics, compare ill with the broader beauties of the Hudson or the finish of the lawns on the Thames.' Mrs Trollope, in *A Visit to Italy* (1842), was even more scathing: 'Many is the canal that I have seen, navigated by coal-barges, incomparably superior in every feature which constitutes the beauty of the landscape, to this miserable little river.'

These commentators were, of course, reporting on a rural society in decline. The stately villas and their rambling outbuildings seemed increasingly anachronistic in a Europe that was fast industrializing. The neglect would continue well into this century, and it is only during the last forty years that any serious effort has been made to restore and maintain this rich architectural heritage. A handful of owners and foreign purchasers kept up their estates, but with four thousand villas standing in north-eastern Italy, the task could only be undertaken by a public body. An organization called the Venetian Villa Corporation was founded in 1958 and in twenty years the corporation and its successors restored over six hundred villas in the Veneto and Friuli regions. It is to this combination of private and state-funded initiatives that we owe a rural landscape that is probably far more attractive today than it was a century ago.

At Oriago you'll see on the left the eighteenth-century Villa Mocenigo, a plain block with a rounded gable, and a hundred metres further on the austere but more graceful sixteenth-century Villa Gradenigo. Mira, at the end of the eighteenth century, was succinctly described by William Beckford as 'a village of palaces'. At its entrance, on the right, is the Villa Widman-Foscari, originally of 1719 but altered during the following century. This villa, tall and compact, is open to the public but is not very rewarding. The interior is frescoed, to be sure, but hung with ghastly chandeliers and filled with mediocre furniture. It does at least give an idea of the kind of decoration and

manipulation of space that the leisured gentry of the Veneto coveted. The outbuildings contain collections of taxidermy and carriages, and in the garden is a motley collection of statues and birds, including peacocks, that have not yet been stuffed.

Across the canal is the austere Villa Valmarana, with a loggia on double columns extending the length of the building. Bear left along the canal and, charmingly located opposite what I take to be a power station, is the Villa Contarini of 1558, also known as Villa dei Leoni, a reference to the two stone lions (copies) seated on the steps and the two more lions perched on the central balcony. The animals are absent from the garden front, which has an arcaded loggia. Along the road to Dolo are more villas on both sides of the water.

Turn left at the sign for Fosso, and turn right immediately after you cross the canal. This back road takes you past some of the grander villas of Fiesso d'Artico and emerges opposite Villa Pisani at Strà. More a palace than a villa, it was commissioned in the mid eighteenth century by one of the most powerful of Venetian families, the Pisani. It's a highly decorative building, crowded with statues and urns and garlands – and scorned by the discerning Beckford for its 'pompous façade'. Four caryatids support the balcony that runs the width of the central bays. Baroque rusticated gateways on either side of the villa give access to the vast park. The interior is frescoed, most notably by G. B. Tiepolo, who covered the ceiling of the ballroom with paintings celebrating the glories of the owners.

The gardens are as lavish as the house: there are shady avenues, statuary, a maze, ponds, a gazebo, pavilions, and fine wrought-iron grilles. A broad waterway leads from the palace to the superb stable block, which in itself is more magnificent than most Veneto villas. Inside, the stalls are separated by columns topped with figurines of prancing horses. For most of its length, the Brenta canal resembles a rich

Villa Foscari at Malcontenta: a powerful villa by Palladio.

suburb with mansions cheek by jowl with more mansions. Here, however, laid out on the grandest scale, is a park where one can wander for hours, although its proximity to Padua means that you are unlikely to find yourself alone. The ice-cream vans parked outside the palace on weekend afternoons will alert you to the presence of Paduans refreshing themselves before and after their afternoon strolls. Nonetheless, in many ways these luxurious gardens are more satisfying than the house.

The villa demonstrates that when it comes to flashy display, the eighteenth century was hard to beat, but the attention to design and workmanship had in many respects declined since Palladio's day. See how the cornices of the side elevation simply fail to join up with the complex pilasters and mouldings of the façade. Nor is the transition of the façade from the pilastered side bays to the half-columns of the central bay of the *piano nobile* any smoother. It's as though two separate structures were merely placed side by side. Still, one mustn't be grudging; Villa Pisani is by any standards a magnificent estate, and outrageously profligate in its use of space, notably in the huge arcades and court-yards of the ground floor, and, of course, the park.

The Pisani family did not own the estate for long. In 1807 Napoleon became the proprietor, though he only spent one night there. In 1934 two other dictators with a taste for excessive grandeur, Mussolini and Hitler, had their first meeting in this very spot. Beyond Villa Pisani is the obelisked Villa Foscarini, and other villas of Noventa Padovana, on the very fringes of Padua.

Skirt round Padua by following signs for Rovigo. After driving a few kilometres down this road (the SS16) you will reach Mandriola, where on the other side of the Battaglia canal you will see Scamozzi's Villa Molin (1597), with its fine pedimented portico. Vincenzo Scamozzi (1552–1616) was Palladio's principal disciple and rival, and a splendid architect in his own right. Follow signs for the Museo dell'Aria. This

museum of aviation is installed in the castle of San Pelagio that once belonged to the Carraresi, the family that rules Padua in medieval times. Its liveliest feature is the machicolated tower, a medieval fragment in a building much altered in the late eighteenth century. Return to the SS16 and head south. Just before Battaglia Terme, another spa, you will see on the other side of the canal the great mass of Cataio, a castellated hulk, architecturally graceless but done up with terraces, turrets, gateposts with statues, and a park. It was built in the 1570s by the Venetian general Pio degli Obizzi, to whom the invention of the howitzer is attributed, and was expanded in the nineteenth century. It became the property of the Dukes of Modena in 1803. With its faintly militaristic air, Cataio is fortunately atypical of the villas of the Veneto. The interior is frescoed by Zelotti but is not open to the public.

Turn right at Battaglia for Carrara San Giorgio and the neighbouring and more interesting village of Carrara San Stefano, the base of the Carraresi. No evidence remains in the village of their power and influence. San Stefano is of interest because it pos-sesses a church and campanile of romanesque origin. On its north wall are a hefty brick canopy and inscriptions, and inside the church a lovely mid fourteenth-century marble tomb by Andreolo de' Santi with beautiful relief figures of the Virgin and Saints. The church also has a virile geometric floor of inlaid marble.

Just south of Battaglia, situated on a hillock, is another villa, the domed Villa Selvatico (or Emo-Capodilista), which is set in a nineteenth-century garden designed by Japelli (1783–1852), whose most celebrated building is the Café Pedrocchi in Padua (see p. 112). The garden was laid out to imitate the journeys of Virgil through Hades, but has become so overgrown that this theme is now difficult to follow. Continue towards Rovigo on the main road. At the next road bridge, cross the canal to look at Villa Emo (1588), set among formal gardens. This splendid Palladian house, with a double staircase rising to the portico of the *piano nobile*, may well be the work of Scamozzi.

Groaning giants supporting the balcony of the vast Villa Pisani at Strà.

Just before Rovigo you cross the River Po, and from now on you are in the Polesine, a flat expanse of large fields reminiscent of the plains north-east of Venice. Canals are threaded in straight lines across the landscape, and only occasional clumps of cypresses or other trees break the broad horizontal expanses. In winter it can be fog-bound for days, bleak and endless. In more clement weather it has a gentle blandness.

Rovigo's main square is Piazza Vittorio Emanuele. At one end is a drab clock-tower, adjoining the town hall with its renaissance loggia. The impressive Palazzo Roncale (1555) to the left of the town hall – rusticated arcades below with grotesque heads in the keystones, and a *piano nobile* marked by fluted Ionic pilasters and a balustrade – is the work of Michele Sammicheli (1484–1559). To the left is the brick expanse of the originally fifteenth-century Palazzo Roverella, grand but monotonous. Also in the piazza is the Pinacoteca, a well displayed picture collection, showing lesser painters such as Nicolò di Pietro Paradisi (*fl.*1394–1430) and Girolamo da Santacroce (1480–1556), as well as the likes of Giovanni Bellini and the Flemish painter Mabuse (*c.*1478–*c.*1533). Tintoretto is represented by four excellent male heads. The silliest painting is a *Deposition* by Domenico Panetti (*c.* 1460–1512), which makes Christ look as if he's being tickled. The paintings by Palma Vecchio (1480–1528) are rather dull, and there is a superabundance of seventeenth-century painters such as Luca Giordano (1632–1705). The best of the later portraits is by G. B. Tiepolo.

Via Cavour, beyond the white column of 1519 now surmounted by a modern winged lion, leads to the battlemented Porta San Bartolomeo, the grandest surviving city gate. If you turn left at the column up Via Maddalena, you soon come to Piazza Garibaldi, with its equestrian statue of the hero.

From the Palazzo Roncale Via Laurenti crosses the main street of Rovigo to the *duomo*. In the choir is a finely wrought and detailed sixteenth-century bronze candlestick by Desiderio da Firenze (though it has

A *palazzo* at Rovigo, the main city of the Polesine.

In Rovigo, a splendid statue of Garibaldi, the liberator of Italy.

also been attributed to Sansovino himself). In the north transept is a *Resurrection* by Palma Giovane (1544–1628). Visible from the main street are the ruins of the early medieval walls and towers of the *castello*, appropriately known as the Due Torri and now set in public gardens. The taller of the two towers, the Torre Dona, dates from 920 and contained the castle dungeons. Far more interesting than the *duomo* is Zamberlan's curious church known as La Rotonda (1594–1602), octagonal and surrounded by broad balustraded colonnades. The tall campanile by Longhena was built half a century later. The interior is splendid, entirely surrounded by bands of grandiloquent, crowded paintings, and between them a band of baroque statues in niches. Above the walls runs a balustraded gallery, behind which are tall windows and gilt pilasters, making the interior seem more like a ballroom than a church. The high altar is equally grandiose.

Continue east to Adria. On one side of the Canale Bianco, which lends a Venetian nuance to the townscape, is the church of Santa Maria Assunta della Tomba. On the left, as you enter, is an early eighth-century stoup. Rather worn, not surprisingly, and embellished with small heads, it is set within an octagonal baptismal font. On the west front a couple of ancient inscriptions are set into the portal and campanile, a reminder of the fact that Adria, which gave its name to the Adriatic – though nowadays it is 24 kilometres inland – is one of the oldest settlements in the Veneto and there was a flourishing civilization here in the fifth century BC, long before Roman times. In those times, Adria was a port, but once the navigable areas silted up, the city fell into a decline and was eventually destroyed in 1482 during Venice's war against Ferrara and had to be rebuilt. Adria's fascinating past can be explored in the archaeological museum, which houses a major collection of Roman, Greek, and Etruscan artefacts. Its prize exhibit is a Gaulish chariot made of iron and dating from the fourth century BC.

On the other side of the canal is the cathedral. Although a dull building, it is worth visiting to see, on the third pier of the north aisle, the fifth-century Coptic bas-relief of the Virgin Mary and the Archangels Michael and Gabriel, compact, with round gaping eyes. In the sacristy the wooden cupboards are carved with life-size caryatids by Giacomo Piazzetta (1683).

From Adria there's a fast road to Chioggia, a plausible substitute for Venice, especially in high season. A Roman foundation, Chioggia is also intersected by canals lined with *palazzi*. Cross into the old town by the two bridges that lead to the little garden square next to the *duomo* (now closed for restoration). Behind the church, based on a seventeenth-century design by Longhena, is its vast fourteenth-century campanile and the contemporaneous Oratorio of San Martino, with its brick octagonal drum and blind arcading. You are now on the Corso, Chioggia's main

The luxuriant interior of Zamberlan's La Rotonda church at Rovigo.

street, which runs parallel to the main canal of the town. This is a delightful street, broad enough to accommodate even holiday crowds, and lined with innumerable cafés, ice cream parlours, and balloon sellers.

A short distance up the Corso on the right is San Giacomo, a church with a lively, garish, neo-classical marble high altar by Aristide Naccari. Turn right by the flagpole and you'll see Santissima Trinità, with its ceiling painted by followers of Tintoretto. Here a bridge offers a fine view of the main canal. Across the bridge is the church of the Filippini (1772). Return to the Corso, where you'll be facing some restored Venetian-gothic *palazzi*. Beyond the neo-classical town hall is the two-storey Granaio building of 1322. Half-way along its façade is a relief of the Madonna by Sansovino, and behind it is the odoriferous fish market along the canal. Continue up the Corso and on the right you'll see San Andrea, and its byzantine campanile, reputedly of the tenth century.

At the top of the Corso, and it's relief to see them, are the quiet, still waters of the lagoon. Cross the Ponte Vigo, the handsome white bridge to the right, which is guarded by stone lions. From here you can see the bright blue fishing boats strewn with nets and tackle and parked along the canal. The fishing boats are not here solely for the pleasure of camera-wielding tourists. Chioggia is one of the best places along the Veneto coast to savour local specialities such as eels, soft-shell crabs, and *seppie* (cuttle-fish).

Continue straight, across another bridge, to San Domenico. In the south aisle is a fine painting of 1520 by Carpaccio, whose work is infrequently seen outside Venice. It depicts a swarthy St Paul being stigmatized in a glade of flowers. There's also a *Deposition* by Leandro Bassano in which Christ takes only a supporting role to the posturing of three saints. And to the left of the choir is a 'Tintoretto', the *Apparition of the Crucifixion*.

Walk back down the canal, a more peaceful route than the bustling Corso. At the next bridge is a ramshackle renaissance *palazzo*. Propped up with beams and crutches, it is evidently in poor condition,

Left The church of Santissima Trinità along a canal at Chioggia.

Above The wild lagoon beneath a glowering sky near Chioggia.

63

yet this only contributes to its great character. Nevertheless there is a fine line between the picturesque and the pile of rubble, and one can only hope that the building remains standing. A few bridges later cross back to the Corso and return to the *duomo*.

Instead of taking the fast main road back to Venice, drive inland to the hamlet of Pontecasale, where Sansovino's palatial Villa Garzoni of 1537–40 strikes a truly distinctive note among the mostly Palladian-style villas of the Veneto. Garzoni is more like a broad pavilion, with its open portico below and open loggia above, and its wide shallow roof. The lovely courtyard is overlooked by a gang of statues posing along the balustrade. This is Sansovino's only villa in the Veneto and thus a most precious survival. Sansovino's best-known building in the region is in Venice: the sumptuous Biblioteca Marciana opposite the Doge's Palace in the Piazzetta (p. 18). Palladio, for one, admired it extravagantly, yet did not use it as a model for his own later structures. Sansovino, consequently, makes a highly individual impression in his few appearances in the Veneto, aiming for a self-consciously aristocratic grandeur rather than for the large-scale but undemonstrative domesticity of the typical Veneto villa. The farm buildings are also impressive but set well away from the villa itself, and the whole estate and its park are surrounded by a lofty crenellated wall. The unashamed grandeur of the conception and its deliberate separation from any agricultural function are in marked contrast to the Palladian notion of the rural villa.

North of here is Piove di Sacco. The Paolo Veneziano that used to hang in the sacristy was stolen; it has been recovered and is now being restored in Rome. Not far from the centre of town is the grand Palazzo Gradeniga, of sixteenth-century origin. Outside Piove di Sacco to the west is the fifteenth-century Sanctuary of Madonna della Grazie. The *Madonna and Child* in the north aisle is attributed, plausibly, to Giovanni Bellini. Adjoining the church are the beautifully maintained cloister and fountain. Continue west to Brugine, where you'll find the late sixteenth-century Villa Roberti, a rather boxy structure with rooms frescoed by Zelotti. From here main roads return you quickly either to Venice or to Padua.

It was at the church at Piove di Sacco that I experienced, as any independent traveller inevitably must, the combined pleasures and frustrations of tourism. I was keen to see the precious fourteenth-century polyptych by Paolo Veneziano, but was not surprised to find the sacristy door firmly shut. There was no sacristan about, so I hunted for a confessional with a light on, indicating occupation by a priest. I

Carvings on the fourteenth-century Granaio buildings, now the fish market, at Chioggia.

Opposite **Some of the most succulent seafood in the Veneto is caught by the Chioggia fishing fleet.**

succeeded, and waited until an impeccably fat churchman had given his blessing to a penitent parishioner. I then approached, asking to see the painting in the sacristy. It was with great glee that the priest responded with a single word: Stolen! He then elaborated on the fate of the painting. Yet he clearly did not want me to leave his church disappointed, and steered me to the north choir aisle and a fine altar-piece of gilt and inlaid marble which, he affirmed, was by Sansovino. There seems no support for this claim, but the priest was in no doubt. From an art-historical point of view, the attribution was doubtful at best, but the altar was beautiful, the priest's welcome as broad as his belly, and the whole visit, despite the absence of the Veneziano, more than worthwhile.

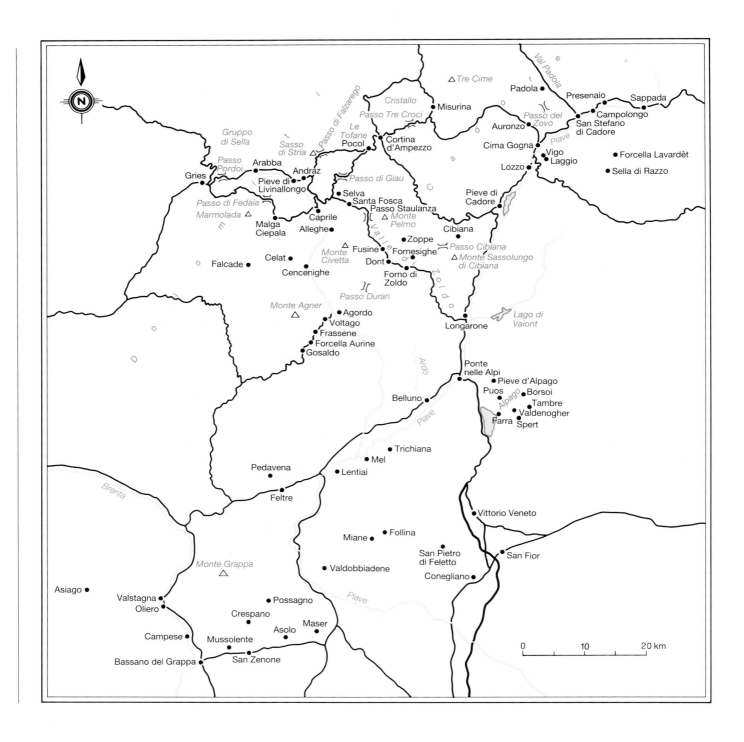

2
From Bassano to the Dolomites

Bassano del Grappa – Feltre – Belluno – Cortina d'Ampezzo – the Cadore –
Conegliano – Asolo

Bassano del Grappa, situated at the spot where the Brenta River emerges from the mountains on to the plains of the Veneto, has, like most of the region's towns, fallen into various hands in the course of its long history. Its thirteenth-century fortifications date from the period when the Ezzelino clan ruled the city. In 1402 it became part of the Venetian empire. Although the town suffered considerable damage during World Wars I and II, it has made a thorough recovery and bustles with activity. I first encountered Bassano as I descended from the Dolomites down the valley of the Brenta. My experience in making the transition from the wintry north to Bassano differed from that noted by William Beckford in 1780, in his *Italy, Spain, and Portugal*: 'About five in the evening we left the country of crags and precipices, of mists and cataracts, and were entering the fertile country of the Bassanese. It was now I beheld groves of olives, and vines clustering the summits of the tallest elms, pomegranates in every garden and vases of citron and orange before almost every door.' Nowadays the vines don't grow on treetops, and although the contrast between the harsh mountains and the lush plain to the south is as marked as ever, the fertility is less evident.

These days Bassano is best known for the production of grappa, a spirit fermented from the pressed skins of grapes, though grappa is also made just about anywhere in Italy that good wine is produced. Boutique grappas from Italy's most distinguished wine estates have in recent years overshadowed the more commercial production of Bassano's distilleries. Those who find grappa too fiery for their taste can indulge, in season, in Bassano's other major speciality: white asparagus. The town is also known for its *forti* biscuits made from cocoa, molasses and spices.

The city's central square is Piazza Libertà, which is surrounded by mostly arcaded and sober old houses, although the neo-classical sprawl of the eighteenth-century church of San Giovanni Battista does rather wreck the intimate scale of the square. From the church steps you can see the customary winged lion on its pedestal and Orazio Marinali's statue of San Bassiano. At the other end of the square is the decorative town hall of 1582 with its clock-face and loggia. The fresco of St Christopher on the façade is attributed to Jacopo Da Ponte, who, with his son Leandro, was the most important painter to emerge from Bassano. Indeed both these sixteenth-century painters are known by the name of the town rather than by their true name of Da Ponte, even though they established their reputations in Venice. To add to the confusion there are a total of five artists in the family: Jacopo is the most important in artistic terms, but you will also encounter canvases by his father Francesco,

A detail from the column in Piazza Libertà at Bassano del Grappa.

and three sons Francesco, Leandro, and Girolamo.

Jacopo Bassano was born in 1508 or 1510 and died in 1592, and accomplished both these rites of passage in the town after which he is named. He studied with his father Francesco (1475–1539), and clearly shows the influence of Mannerist painters such as Pordenone. He was an adaptable painter, soaking up influences and stylistic trends. He does not have the immediately identifiable hallmarks of other great painters of the Venetian school, such as Veronese. Nonetheless he was a fine painter, accomplished and dramatic in style, and Bassano is, other than Venice, the best place to see his work. Of his sons, Francesco (1549–92) and Leandro (1557–1622) were the most accomplished. Francesco acquired a reputation for domestic and rural scenes, while Leandro was best known as a portraitist.

To the right of the church, Via San Bassiano leads into Piazza Garibaldi, where you will find the brick fourteenth-century church of San Francesco. Its west front is extended by a baldacchino porch. The interior is plain and, by Italian standards, unadorned. Adjoining the church to the south is a pretty renaissance cloister, and its monastic buildings now house the Museo Civico, which has very fine coin and ceramics collections. Jacopo Bassano is represented here by two exceptional paintings, notably the *Baptism of St Lucilla* (1568). Here too is a very fine fourteenth-century painted Crucifix by Guariento di Arpo. In addition the museum possesses 2000 drawings and designs by Canova, and an exceptionally large library.

On leaving the museum or church you will find yourself opposite one of Bassano's more stylish cafés, from where there is a good view of the thirteenth-century Torre di Ezzelino. Return to Piazza Libertà. Near the statue of the saint an archway leads into Piazzetta Monte Vecchio, where you will see a number of houses with painted façades and the fifteenth-century Monte di Pietà, which looks as if it has been taken apart and incorrectly reassembled. Return once more to Piazza Libertà and take Via Matteotti alongside the town hall, passing on the right the baroque façade of the former church of Madonna del Patrocinio. Cross the little piazza at the top of the street, and walk through the gateway next to another medieval tower. You are now in the castle compound of the Ezzelini, though only a few walls and two towers survive. Here too is the *duomo*, its campanile a recycling of one of the towers. The cathedral, rebuilt in the sixteenth century, has a handsome interior, with a rather heavy cornice and balustrade encircling the entire space. Marinali, the sculptor responsible for San Bassiano in Piazza Libertà, also carved the highly competent statues in the south chapel. The many Leandro Bassano paintings within the *duomo* are inferior to the delicate *Nativity* by his father Jacopo in the north-east chapel.

Return to the top of Via Matteotti and turn right down Via Gamba, which leads to Bassano's famous wooden bridge, the Ponte degli Alpini. Its original

The stylish town-hall clock at Bassano del Grappa.

Stylish eighteenth-century ornament on the former church of the Madonna del Patrocinio, Bassano del Grappa.

precursor was built in 1209, and it has often been rebuilt since; the present bridge still reflects Palladio's design of 1569. The best view of it is from the major road bridge just south of here, but from the wooden bridge itself you can see the charming old balconied houses that back on to the greeny waters of the Brenta. The streets on both sides of the bridge are lined with shops selling the primary local products: grappa, ceramics and, in season, asparagus. For the pleasure of the view, bear left on returning to terra firma from the bridge and you will emerge on Piazza Terraglio, high above the river.

Bassano is perhaps less rich in major sights than some other towns of comparable size in the Veneto, but it has an easy, unpretentious charm of its own. It is accessible, friendly, and far from unsophisticated. There are few indications today that just north of here, on the plateau around Asiago and on the slopes of

Monte Grappa, some of the most bitter fighting of World War I took place, until the Italians eventually triumphed over the Austrians. The Italians have not forgotten the terrible price they paid for that victory, and there are impressive war memorials to be seen near Asiago and on Monte Grappa, as well as close to Bassano itself.

Drive north out of Bassano up the Brenta valley, which is quite dramatic in places. Rather than taking the main Trento road, take the road on the other side of the river. Overlooking the village of Campese is a supposedly tenth-century chapel of San Martino, obviously much rebuilt. The church is locked but the keyhole shows frescoes within. The larger church closer to the river was once part of a Benedictine monastery, and a dilapidated cloister survives. In a chapel alongside the choir is a small funerary chapel containing a neo-classical plaque dated 1543, a bust, and a mosaic inscription. The church also contains some good altar-pieces and a fresco of the Crucifixion. Further north at Oliero, the church of San Spirito is said to be thirteenth-century, but the exterior looks five centuries later. Valstagna straggles along stone terraces set into the cliffs that tower above the Brenta.

Continue up the valley and bear right on to the Belluno road, which will bring you to Feltre. Of prehistoric origins, Feltre was colonized by the Romans. After 1404 it became subservient to Venice, and lost out in the war against the League of Cambrai, and was sacked in 1509–10. Almost all the buildings in the old town date from the Venetian rebuilding that took place during the decades after the disaster, giving the town a degree of uniformity unusual in the cities of the Veneto. The old town is ranged along a ridge above the more commercial parts of the town. Among the buildings outside the old town is the church of Ognissanti, which apparently contains a *Transfiguration* which is the masterpiece of the best-known local painter, Lorenzo Luzzo (1467–1612), more commonly

The wooden bridge at Bassano has crossed the River Brenta for centuries.

known as Morto da Feltre. Unfortunately the church is in dangerous condition and has for some time been closed to visitors.

By following signs for the Centro Storico, you will reach a gateway that takes you up along the spine of the city, Via Mezzaterra, past dozens of sixteenth-century houses with long eaves, rounded windows, square balconies and, often, painted façades. On the right is the church of San Giacomo, which has a fine renaissance portal, and no. 15A on the left has robust carved wooden doors. Small squares and gardens break the line of mansions climbing the hill. At the top on the right is the massive Palazzo del Comune, with its rusticated arcades and balustrade; it has been attributed, probably falsely, to Palladio. An immense winged lion in relief gazes out over the entrance. The comedies of the still-admired Venetian dramatist Goldoni were first performed here in the eighteenth century, and a century later a theatre, still in existence, was constructed upstairs. In the adjoining town hall is a splendid chamber with frescoes of Venetian governors' coats of arms and a charmingly painted ceiling.

Emerge again into Piazza Maggiore. This pleasantly ramshackle square is on three levels. On the central one stand a column with the winged lion of Venice, a flagpole, and two nineteenth-century statues. Above stands the church of San Rocco (1599), and two towers that survive from the castle destroyed in 1510. Between the steps leading to the church is a broad panelled fountain of 1520 by Tullio Lombardo (c.1455–1532). The grandiose *palazzo* in Venetian-gothic style is nineteenth-century. The continuation of Via Mezzaterra is Via Luzzo, also lined with frescoed houses (no. 3 is especially charming). At the end of the street is the Museo Civico, which combines archaeological exhibits with paintings by Giovanni Bellini, Cima da Conegliano, Palma Giovane, and Francesco Maffei (1675–1755).

By the side of the town hall an arcaded staircase descends the slope. You will emerge by the rustic apse

Below Santi Vittore e Corona near Feltre, in the foothills of the Dolomites.

of the baptistery, which presents more elegant aspects with the renaissance south portal and the seventeenth-century loggia at the west end. Just beyond it is the *duomo*. By the east entrance is a late fifteenth-century stone effigy, back against the wall. The sixteenth-century arcades conceal more ancient foundations, notably the long narrow medieval crypt and the choir, where there is a very fine tomb by Tullio Lombardo (1528). In the north-east corner stands a massive if battered early medieval stone bishop's throne.

Although much of the Veneto is wine country, there's a brewery in the village of Pedavena just to the north of Feltre. Pedavena is a kind of villa suburb these days, and its most striking building is the grandly frivolous seventeenth-century Villa Luciani. South of Feltre, perched above the Treviso road, is the sanctuary of Santi Vittore e Corona (1096). Many of the medieval frescoes with which the interior is abundantly decorated are sadly faded. In the galleried choir reposes the marble sarcophagus of the two martyrs, a gift of the Holy Roman Emperor Charles IV. As in the *duomo*, a massive but crude early medieval bishop's throne is placed near the choir. To the left of the choir is an elaborate gothic tabernacle, also well preserved. The adjoining fifteenth-century cloister, filled with shrubbery, is delightful, and on the west side frescoes depict the construction of the martyrs' tomb and views of Feltre.

The road east of Feltre follows the valley of the Piave, and the frequent villages along the valley floor and slopes are flanked by wild hills to the south and the first wall of the Dolomites to the north. One of the most interesting villages is Lentiai, on account of its unexpectedly lovely church, with graceful arcades and a splendid coffered ceiling (1570), each large square panel painted by Cesare Vecellio (c. 1521–1601), who also painted some of the altar-pieces. In the north aisle is a *Baptism* by Palma Giovane, full of movement, and a *Madonna and Saints* by the sixteenth-century painter Giovanni da Mel, who takes his name from a village further up the valley. A few kilometres beyond Lentiai, a road leads south to the isolated hilltop castle of Zumelle, which has the first peaks of the Dolomites

Left The lion of St Mark keeps an eye on the Piazza Maggiore in Feltre.

Above Inside the romanesque church of Santi Vittore e Corona near Feltre.

as a superb backdrop. The earliest stones of this fortress date from the eighth century, but the interior, much reconstructed, is disappointing. The countryside here is especially lovely, a braid of high meadows and deep wooded dells.

Mel is a pleasant town with some pretensions to grandeur. Around the main square are old mansions, many with tall tiled chimney-pots. In the north aisle of the parish church is an old if not especially distinguished altar-piece of the Virgin and saints (1531) by Giovanni da Mel. Drive eastward from Mel, and cross the river near Trichiana and head north to the Certosa di Vedana, a large monastery enclosed within square walls of peeling lemon-coloured stucco. The Certosa, founded in 1155 but mostly of later construction, is prettily set against the first ranges of the Dolomites, but is closed to visitors, as it is the preserve of the closed Carthusian order.

The drive to Belluno, situated at the junction of the rivers Piave and Ardo, becomes increasingly grand, as the Dolomite ranges that enclose the city loom into view. It's best to leave the car at the Palasport, where you will find ample free parking just a short walk from the centre. Belluno presents a fairly modern aspect until one reaches Piazza del Duomo, which is dominated by the amply moulded eighteenth-century campanile. The cathedral was designed by Tullio Lombardo but largely rebuilt subsequently. The west front is a weird mixture of styles (parts of the earlier gothic church were incorporated) that does not augur well, but the interior is far more satisfactory, with its barrel-vaulted nave, lofty renaissance arcades, and domed crossing. In the south aisle is an altar-piece by Cesare Vecellio which depicts Piazza del Duomo. The last chapel in the south aisle near the choir has a tender altar-piece of the Deposition by Palma Giovane. At the same spot in the north aisle is a door that leads down to the crypt, where the altar, a reused sarcophagus, has a charming fourteenth-century alabaster panel of the Madonna and Child below, and above it an early but crude fifteenth-century polyptych.

On leaving the cathedral you'll see the sixteenth-century baptistery, rebuilt in the last century. The statue of John the Baptist on the font cover is by Andrea Brustolon, and the *Madonna and Child* behind the altar is a fifteenth-century image much revered by pious Bellunesi.

Behind the fountain (1532) in the centre of the square is the finest building in Belluno, the Palazzo dei Rettori, where the Venetian governors once resided; their busts still stare out into space from the palace's façade. Begun in 1491 in an ultra-sophisticated Venetian-renaissance style, the *palazzo's* generous number of windows are beautifully carved. In niches of varying designs are the busts, and also heraldic devices and medallions. Two lavish balconies dominate the centre of the building. The ground floor is a sturdily arcaded loggia. The clock-tower, faced with pink marble, was added in 1549, and to the right rises the Torre Civica, the sole remnant of the medieval bishop's palace.

In the small piazza opposite the cathedral is the Museo Civico, located in a seventeenth-century *palazzo*. The ground floor is devoted to archaeological displays. Upstairs are paintings by Sebastiano Ricci (1659–1734), who was born in Belluno, Cesare Vecellio and Bartolommeo Montagna (c.1450–1523); the eloquent Brustolon is represented by a small, intensely carved Crucifix. More of his carvings may be seen in the church of San Pietro, just off Via Mezzaterra.

On leaving the museum turn right into the charming Piazza del Mercato. Behind the early fifteenth-century fountain is the Monte di Pietà, built a century later, with a tiny representation of the Pietà above the central grilled window. Leading off the square is Via Mezzaterra, which gently slopes southwards, flanked by gothic and renaissance mansions. North of the piazza is the similarly endowed Via Rialto, leading to the sixteenth-century Porto Doiana, which retains its large wooden gates. Turn right down the arcaded Via Roma, and you will find on the right the church of San Stefano, prefaced by another renaissance fountain. The south wall of the church is pierced by gothic lancets. The south portal is a splendid mid fifteenth-century assembly, brought here from another church, consisting of statues on corbels and pinnacles, and a

An imposing doorway in Piazza del Duomo at Belluno.

canopied statue of the Virgin Mary. The lovely interior has tall gothic arcades over robust capitals, and a complex rib-vaulted choir. In the south-east chapel are excellent frescoes (c.1587) by Jacopo da Montagnana, and the tender gilt altar-piece, in an early renaissance style, is by Andrea di Foro. Brustolon carved the slender Crucifix in the north aisle.

From Belluno drive north-east to Ponte nelle Alpi, where a flamboyant castellated mock-castle guards the banks of the Piave. Sixteen kilometres north of here is Longarone, which was almost destroyed in October 1963 at 10.42 p.m. precisely, when a landslide in the Vaiont valley caused floods that swept away houses and churches and killed almost 1500 people. The village has been reconstructed with a little imagination, though unfortunately the busy main road bisects it. The new village is clustered around a fine modern church by Giovanni Michelucci, built entirely of concrete and surrounded by swirling ramps. In a kind of open-air crypt alongside the church is a memorial to those who died. Although the photographs and architectural relics displayed here clearly show how utterly devastating the flood waters must have been, the rebirth of the town testifies to the resilience of the local people. Since hardly a single family can have been unaffected by the onslaught of water and mud, it must have taken remarkable determination to rebuild Longarone and settle again in the once devastated valley. Only a couple of decades after the tragedy, there is only the slightly puzzling phenomenon of a bright modern town in an otherwise ancient land to betray the fact that something terrible once happened here.

Driving north up the Piave valley, the Dolomites become more and more prominent. Visitors to the major cities of the Veneto plain easily forget that one third of the region's 18,000 square kilometres is mountainous. These dramatic mountains were named after the French nobleman, Marquis Déodat de Gratet de Dolomieu (1750–1801), who first identified their geological structure. The term soon became commonly used, and John Murray used it constantly in his guidebooks in the nineteenth century. They are spectacular mountains, wonderfully untidy and unpredictable. Indeed, it is often difficult to identify peaks or groups because so fantastical are their rock formations that they change shape according to where they are viewed from. All mountains do, but the Dolomites play more tricks of this sort than most.

Cortina d'Ampezzo, north-west of Longarone, is the principal town of the Dolomite region, and remarkably pleasant it is too. Traffic circles the town, leaving the main street, Corso Italia, to pedestrians. The otherwise unremarkable eighteenth-century church contains an ornate altar-piece by Brustolon. The white campanile, a nineteenth-century contribution, is fairly ugly, but acts as a focal point for the town. There is the inevitable urban sprawl, but the chalet style of building means that the outskirts are less hideous than in most Veneto towns. Much of the building is fairly recent, as a fire in 1976 destroyed many older structures. The Posta is the smart hotel, and the bar is a favourite gathering place for the trendy set every evening around seven.

Cortina has night-life and smart shops, but it also has prices to match. Even the pizzerias are expensive, extracting full fare for the privilege of rubbing shoulders with the rich and the glamorous. Other, more modest resorts such as Arabba, Misurina, Forno di Zoldo, or Malga Ciapela, all offer splendid opportunities for summer hikes and winter sports. If you want greater isolation and can do without a disco within walking distance, remember that on top of every mountain pass there will be at least one hotel, and that the Dolomites are dotted with *rifugi*, mountain huts that are far more sophisticated than their nomenclature suggests. Wherever you roam in the Dolomites, you will never be thirsty or hungry. There are many well-maintained mountain tracks, some over 150 km long, as well as many additional local itineraries. These are the best ways to find and observe the wildlife of the Dolomites, which includes white partridges (the only birds that turn white in winter), the red-eyebrowed mountain pheasant, and roebuck and chamois.

From Cortina take the road for Misurina, which offers superb views of the barbarous, awesome mass of Cortina's principal mountain, the Cristallo. Cross the Passo Tre Croci (1809 m), and shortly thereafter bear left for Misurina. You will soon see broadly spaced but dramatic towers of stone on the horizon, some like thimbles protruding into the sky, others more rugged as they rise in a series of shelves of ever diminishing size until they reach their prickly apex. The lake at Misurina is surrounded by hotels and restaurants, and a home for asthmatic children. Immediately after the resort, a fork leads to Rifugio Auronzo at the base of the Tre Cime, one of the bleaker and most dramatic of Dolomite complexes.

The road to the *rifugio* is a cul de sac, so an alternative is to ignore the fork to Misurina, and to stay on the main road, which continues through pine forests to Auronzo. This is a long sprawling town, well equipped with *pensioni* and restaurants, but the sawmills along the river don't enhance the atmosphere. The only landmark is the medieval but much restored campanile. From the cold octagonal neo-classical church at the south end of the town, turn left along a road that twists up to Passo del Zovo, where the scenery takes a turn for the better, with views of the broad wooded flanks of Val Padola. Descending the pass, you will see on the right the charming white-washed chapel of Santa Anna (1699) with its tiny belfry. A little further on you reach Padola with its impressive modern campanile; a plaque records how a worker fell to his death during its construction. Just after Padola take the turn to San Stefano. At San Nicolò di Comelico every inch of the choir of the little gothic church is covered with slightly faded late fifteenth-century frescoes by Giovanni Francesca da Tolmezzo. The whole is greater than the sum of its parts. The road continues to the uninspiring little town of San Stefano di Cadore, where the Padola river joins the Piave. It's worth entering the hideous and gloomy church to see the refined seventeenth-century altar-piece studded with scenes from the Passion carved in white marble. San Stefano is the main town of the upper Piave valley, which is known as the Cadore, and before 1918 most of it was Austrian territory. The older inhabitants still speak a Ladino dialect, and German-speaking visitors would feel perfectly at home here. Nonetheless the Germanic character of much of the Cadore is less marked than in the Alto Adige, or South Tyrol, to the west of the Veneto Dolomites. The green Loden jackets, feathered hats and knee breeches of the South Tyrol won't be encountered much here.

From here take the Sappada road, which follows the Piave. At Campolongo is an octagonal neo-classical church with a charming interior. The drabness of the roadside tends to obscure the prettiness of the mountain slopes, so it's worth crossing the river along the road to Forcella Lavardêt. Where the houses end, look back at the steep meadows above the village; beneath the dark pine forests, old chalets and haylofts with wooden overhangs are dotted among the pastures, evidence of the intensity with which every scrap of

The jagged peaks of the Tre Cime.

A statue in Pieve di Cadore honouring Titian, who was born here in about 1477.

cultivable or grazing land is employed. Return to the Sappada road. After Presenaio the valley narrows, then broadens at Sappada, a pleasant if sprawling resort village. The eighteenth-century church of Santa Margarita is finely proportioned, and architectural ornaments – pilasters and window mouldings – are painted in *trompe-l'œil* manner on to the façade in a dramatic peach colour. Return to San Stefano and follow signs for Pieve de Cadore. The first stretch of the road brings you to Cima Gogna, and here you bear left to Laggio.

Just off the road to Sella di Razzo at the edge of Laggio – it's easy to miss it – a lane to the right leads to the thirteenth-century chapel of Santa Margarita. This tiny church once stood alone in the fields overlooking the village, but now it is abutted by modern houses and chalets. The chapel itself is unremarkable, but inside are vivid medieval frescoes of fine quality depicting scenes from the life of the saint.

In the nearby village of Vigo, the parish church stands shoulder to shoulder with the chapel of Santa Maria della Difesa, which apparently has abundant frescoes, but both churches were resolutely locked when I visited. Fortunately the attractions of the fourteenth-century church of Santa Orsola, in the little piazza below the parish church, are exterior and take the form of asymmetrical fifteenth-century frescoes on the façade; they are of middling quality. From Vigo follow the signs for Pieve, and rejoin the Piave valley at Lozzo. At the entrance to Pieve there is a good view of the long slender reservoirs that fill the valley floor. The main square of Pieve gathers around a modern statue of Titian, who was born here in 1477 (or later, depending on which scholar you believe – some say as late as 1490). The sombre town hall of grey stone with its ungainly battlemented tower dates from the fifteenth century, but was rebuilt in 1525. The parish church just above the square contains the town's only painting by Titian, a *Madonna and Saints*. Just off the square is the supposed birthplace of Titian. The story may be untrue, but the stone house is very pretty, with its immense overhanging roof, and its balcony, staircase and shutters, all of weathered wood. There is a small museum inside the house, and an archaeological museum in the town hall.

From Pieve take the Cortina road, and after about 13 km turn left along the road towards Forno. You will soon come to Cibiana, a village that is proud of the modern murals that adorn the houses in the quaint core of the village. This pride is unmerited. The road climbs up to the Passo Cibiana (1530 m); from the Rifugio Rimauro there are lovely views on to sheer rock faces and the peaks of Monte Sassolungo opposite. Shortly afterwards you will pass Fornesighe; its upper terraces are crowded with old chalets, their wooden balconies perilously angled and rickety. Forno di Zoldo is the main resort village of the wooded Valle di Zoldo, much

Paint masquerades as stone on the façade of Santa Margarita at Sappada.

17· S· MARGARITA 79

loved by German tourists. From here a road winds north to Zoppe (1450 m), which has some impressive older stone chalets and some weathered but very beautiful haylofts, constructed from dark caramel wood raised above a stone base, with bands of latticework openings on to the storerooms. Behind Zoppe rises the stark stony hand of Monte Pelmo (3168 m), and from the village there are splendid views on to the crags of the Dolomites, although one is less enveloped in the mountains here than further north around Cortina.

From Forno, take the road to Dont and Agordo. From Dont the road climbs relentlessly up towards the Passo Duran. The pass is only 1605 m, but feels higher, especially as one descends along what is for much of the way a single-track road to the relatively low-lying town of Agordo. If you dare to take your eyes off the road for more than two seconds, you will enjoy superb views of the mountains. Agordo itself, surrounded by high mountains but less oppressively than in more northerly Dolomite resorts, is a pleasant, easygoing town. Its large main square is dominated by the two towers of its coarse nineteenth-century church. But the church interior is more rewarding, with some renaissance paintings, including two by Palma Giovane. The most interesting building in the square is in the opposite corner, the Palazzo Manzoni, an inflated villa of considerable panache in a not always authentic seventeenth-century style.

From Agordo you can make a rewarding circuit to the south by following signs for Gosaldo. This route is free of tourist attractions, and tourists in any numbers, but full of visual delight. You will soon find yourself climbing into the hills overlooking the town and entering a landscape that combines all the finest features of the Dolomites: steep meadows, pine forests, and peaks askew in all their chaotic splendour on the horizon. Drive through the pleasant villages of Voltago and Frassene, which are both on the flanks of the hefty massif of Monte Agner. The road rises to 1300 m at

The colours of winter near Caprile.

Forcella Aurine before descending to Gosaldo. From here take the left turn marked Agordo; this road curves high above a very deep valley, and then gently drops back to Agordo a few kilometres further on.

From Agordo drive north up the Cordevole valley to Cencenighe. The church here contains a portrait of St Anthony by Tizianello (1570–c. 1650) set within an elaborate altar-piece topped with rustic statues that forms a charming ensemble. By the church take the turning marked Falcade. Pass through the rural settlement of Celat, and turn right when you see the sign for San Simon. This romanesque church is set on a steep slope surrounded by woods and distinguished by its tall slender tower and spire. Those lucky enough to find the church open will see within some sixteenth-century frescoes by Paris Bordone; those compelled to remain outside can at least admire the ravishing view. Return to Cencenighe and continue northwards to Alleghe, a lovely lakeside resort against the backdrop of the gnarled Dolomite peaks of Monte Civetta. The pretty church has rococo tendencies and is worth a glance, as is the excellent *pasticceria* next door.

Continue up the road towards Caprile, and bear left for Malga Ciepala. You will soon come to the village of Rocca Pietore, which has a gothic church. Malga Ciepala is a pleasant resort at the foot of the highest range in the Dolomites, Marmolada (3342 m). A cable car ascends the *massif*, and in winter ski lifts tie into a network that links up with other Dolomite resorts. The road now leaves the Veneto briefly after crossing the steep Passo di Fedaia (2057 m), blessed with splendid views of the Marmolada range. At Gries bear right along the twisting road that takes you over the Passo Pordoi and thus back into the Veneto and on to the resort of Arabba, with its complex of ski lifts and mountain paths. Beyond Arabba the road calms down, and brings you to the hamlet of Pieve, with its elegant church tower and surprisingly grand houses, firewood neatly stacked beneath them, bunched tightly together on a spur overlooking a deep valley.

Beyond Andraz the road begins to twist its way up a series of seventeen hairpins. On your left you will see the ruins of Castello d'Andraz perched on top of an

83

Throughout the Dolomites, as here at Arabba,
roadside shrines offer comfort to travellers.

immense boulder, and on the horizon is the Sella range.
As you climb up towards the Passo di Falzarego, the
skyline begins to resemble a particularly alarming
reading on an ECG machine. From the top of the
pass you begin the descent towards Pocol and Cortina. In clear weather there are splendid views of the
Tofane *massif*, the highest of the ranges encircling
Cortina, and the Sasso di Stria; its jagged peaks cap
immense cliffs.

Those with an unquenchable appetite for Dolomite
roads and landscapes might wish to delay their return
to Cortina by turning right at Pocol and crossing the
Passo di Giau (2236 m), which in my experience is one
of the most tricky Dolomite passes, dotted with icy
patches long after other passes are clear of such
hazards. Continue past Selva to Santa Fosca, where the
façade of the late-gothic parish church is embellished
with a huge fresco of St Christopher, rustic but
forceful. The road continues to Forcella Staulanza at

the base of Monte Pelmo. Here a wilder landscape
comes into view, and on an autumn afternoon the
setting sun illumines the rock faces with vivid shades
of bronze, mauve and pink, an effect for which the
Dolomites, with their receptive limestone, are justly
celebrated. At Fusine the parish church is prettily
decorated with faded frescoes of no great distinction,
but the overall effect has some charm. The road will
lead you along the flanks of Monte Pelmo to Dont and
Forno, from which you can bear north-east towards
Cibiana and the main road back to Cortina, or south-
east to Longarone and Belluno.

Just south of Ponte Nelle Alpi, where the road turns
off to Belluno, you can continue south for about two
kilometres, then turn left in the direction of Pieve to
explore the Alpago region. To be sure, this region of
gentle mountains is small fry after the Dolomites, but it
does have attractions of its own, on a more modest, and
less crowded, scale. Pieve itself, somewhat overshadowed by the jagged peaks to the north, fights back
with a tall stone campanile. Borsoi and Puos are quite
imposing villages, with attractive stone houses along
winding streets; and the small town of Tambre, 1000 m
up, has some handsome chalets. Descend steeply
through Spert and Valdanogher towards Farra, and
rejoin the main road south near Lago di Santa Croce.

Continue to Vittorio Veneto, an ungainly urban
sprawl, with the older sections of the town on the
slopes to the west. The sprawl is made up of two
overlapping communities, Ceneda and Serravalle. The
towns were keen rivals until Italian reunification
prompted them to embrace permanently and adopt
their triumphalist joint name. The more northerly,
Serravalle, is also the more interesting, and its old
quarter lies close to the main road. The eighteenth-
century *duomo* contains an altar-piece by Titian of
1547. Opposite the south door is Via Casoni, with a
number of renaissance mansions, but there is even
finer architecture across the bridge, where you will
find a piazza. Here, facing the water, is a house with

The onion-domed steeple at Andraz.

the most irregular arcades I have ever seen. On the far side of the square is the slender tower, decorated with heraldic devices, of the fifteenth-century arcaded loggia which now houses the local museum. The trefoiled fenestration of the loggia is delightful, and there is, for once, an unconventional polychrome representation in low relief of that ubiquitous winged lion. To the left of the loggia is the narrow Via Martiri della Libertà, with a superb, if very crowded and sometimes gloomy, collection of gothic and renaissance *palazzi*.

A few kilometres to the south is Ceneda. At the top of its main square in the old centre is an attractive fountain and a small park of chestnut trees. The eighteenth-century cathedral has a fine neo-classical interior of mottled grey marble. Although richly furnished, it contains few items of interest. In the south aisle is a two-dimensional *Madonna and Saints* (1508) by Jacopo da Valenza. On emerging you'll see on the right the sixteenth-century loggia; upstairs is a museum commemorating the battle of Vittorio Veneto. High above the town are the remains of the ancient castle of San Martino.

South-east of here is the village of San Fior. Within its hideous neo-byzantine church is a masterly polyptych by Cima da Conegliano, with its striking main panel depicting John the Baptist. In the north transept is a small taut Crucifix carved by Brustolon.

From here it is a short drive south-west to Conegliano. The main street, Via XX Settembre, slowly curves around the old town. Below a gigantic fifteenth-century campanile is the entrance to the *duomo*, not at all obvious as it consists of an elegant renaissance portal set into a wall behind a stylish arcade of pointed arches. The triple-windowed façade of this loggia is adorned with a fresco cycle (1595) by Pozzoserrato. This apparently secular self-presentation is explained by the alliance of the *duomo* with the Scuola di Santa Maria dei Battuti, a thirteenth-century fraternity of flagellants, of which the *duomo* (not a true cathedral) is

The stone supports of the canal at Vittorio Veneto.

the associated church. Conegliano suffered gravely from bomb damage during World War II, but for the most part the reconstruction and restoration was skilfully undertaken – except here. The church does contain a marvellous altar-piece by Cima da Conegliano, a most lyrical *Sacra conversazione* of 1493, which was commissioned by the Scuola. The frescoes on the nave pillars are contemporaneous, but grossly unsophisticated compared to Cima's work. A painting by Palma Giovane above the west door is too dimly lit to be appreciated.

From the courtyard of the church a staircase leads to the Scuola's Sala dei Battuti, the flagellants' headquarters, with its sixteenth-century frescoes. On leaving the church turn left. At Piazza Cima, turn left again and follow the signs for Cima's house; in the course of its reconstruction, some twelfth-century foundations were excavated. The museum itself, sadly, is not very illuminating. Return to the main road. No. 75 Via XX Settembre has a lovely courtyard and loggia; no. 128,

Intimidating cliffs loom over Passo di Falzarego.

Casa Longega, incorporates a kind of fifteenth-century lapidary museum on its façade, and the arcades are richly carved. The road leads down to the town gate, embellished on the outside with a painting of the winged lion.

From Piazza Cima a steep road leads up past villas to the piazza of Castelvecchio. A century ago the view must have been glorious; now the piazza overlooks the industrialized plains. Formal gardens are planted around the surviving towers of the castle. The principal tower is now the local museum, and contains a large painting by Palma Giovane, and an *Annunciation* by Cima and his pupils. An important fresco by Pordenone that used to be here has been moved to the library on Via XX Settembre.

From Conegliano head north-west to the village of San Pietro di Feletto. The road passes through the vineyards planted with grapes used to make *prosecco*, a highly acceptable sparkling wine, much of which finds its way to the bars of Venice. The church at San Pietro is quite remarkable. It is sheltered on two sides by a crude wooden portico, which protects some early medieval frescoes. One of them, depicting Christ surrounded by implements and vessels and signs of the zodiac, is usually interpreted as Jesus in his role of protector of the arts and crafts. The interior of this plainly constructed romanesque church is also frescoed, much of it in a vaguely byzantine style of considerable narrative and pictorial power. In the apse is a powerful *Christ in Majesty* that could easily date from the twelfth century, and the excellent nave frescoes, which exude great spiritual intensity, are early too. Those in the north aisle are later, possibly fifteenth-century, but have similar complexity and greater visual immediacy. This little church is one of the most fascinating and precious in the northern Veneto.

Drive west to Follina, where there is another major church: a Cistercian abbey of twelfth-century foundation, though the finely proportioned interior with its tall pointed arcades over varied capitals is evidence of a reconstruction a century later. The abbey is overlooked by a superb brick campanile. The high altar is adorned with a complex and lavish late gothic altar-piece that incorporates a polyptych and what is claimed to be an eleventh-century image of the Madonna and Child. The sixteenth-century fresco of the Madonna and saints in the south aisle is a routine effort by Francesco da Milano; nearby hangs a realistic eighteenth-century carved Crucifix. The superb romanesque cloisters of 1268 are enriched with double columns, and heavier single columns with ingenious patterned carving. The old fountain still splashes away, and adjoining the cloister is the ancient refectory. Beyond the cloister is another arcade of 1535, giving access to the pilgrims' lodgings and two goldfish ponds. On leaving the church, walk along Via Pallede, parallel to the west front. It's full of attractive old houses – not the mansions of Belluno or Bassano, but solid unpretentious houses of varied design.

The road from Follina through Miane to Valdobbiadene is especially lovely, passing through hills and hillocks thickly planted with vines. Valdobbiadene is, indeed, a major centre of production for the superior *prosecco* known as Cartizze. The eighteenth-century church here houses, in its south aisle, a fine altar-piece of John the Baptist and saints by Palma Giovane. The other painting in this aisle, almost as good, is by Paris Bordone. But good altar-pieces are common enough in the northern Veneto, so there's a strong case for heading instead for the Bar Alpino or one of the other bars around the main square, where a selection of local *prosecchi* is always available.

Cross the river Piave and drive south to Maser, and the delightful Villa Barbaro, designed by Palladio in the late 1550s. Originally built, as the name suggests, for a leading member of the Barbaro family, it subsequently became the property of the last doge of Venice, Lodovico Manin. The villa itself is quite small, but it is given grandeur by Vittoria's heavily decorated pediment and its four Ionic half-columns, and the buildings as a whole acquire amplitude from the two

A wealth of medieval narrative on the frescoed vaults at the church of San Pietro di Feletto.

broad agricultural wings (barchesses) and from the flanking pavilions, at the same height as the villa, with their sundials. Down on the main road is one of Palladio's two last designs, the Tempietto of 1580, which was not completed until after his death. (The other is the Teatro Olimpico in Vicenza; see p. 142) Although a nod of homage towards the Pantheon, this chapel (unlike the Tempio in Possagno, another version of this distinguished model) is a highly original work, not beautiful, to be sure, but taut and compact, with a sense of reined-in power. Yet blended into the composition is the somewhat frivolous feature of carved garlands strewn between the portico capitals.

The interior of the Villa Barbaro is quite wonderful. Most of the surfaces of the *piano nobile* were frescoed by Veronese, and Alessandro Vittoria was responsible for stucco work such as fireplaces. These decorations were probably in place by 1561. The main hall is enlivened with enchanting paintings of musicians and *trompe l'œil* effects of children appearing to enter the hall. The delicate pastel colours depicting idealized classical landscapes, the white stucco doorways, the breeze through the open windows that look on to the real landscape outside, all contribute to the overall impression of lightness. Blending with Vittoria's decorations are the stucco columns and cornices and doorframes painted most probably by Veronese's younger brother, Benedetto Caliari (1538–98). Combined with the classical allegories is a cheerful sense of the grotesque, whether in the form of the distorted faces over the fireplaces, or the flabby-breasted half-figures painted above the cornices. Veronese reserved his greatest effort for the main hall, the Sala dell'Olimpo. Over painted balconies lean members of the Barbaro family, nonchalant, given effortless command of their home by means of Veronese's brushstrokes. Despite the richness and lavishness of these decorations, there is no hint of the vulgarity that mars so many other decorative schemes of later centuries.

Some of the Veneto's loveliest cloisters at the Cistercian abbey at Follina.

Above The grapes from Valdobbiadene will be used to make Cartizze, the Veneto's best sparkling wine.

Right Palladio's last work, the awesome Tempietto at Maser.

Behind the house is Vittoria's lavish nymphaeum, a swoop of yellow stucco, its niches packed with statues. In the centre a grotto, situated at the foot of a slope of mature conifers and shrubs, curves around a pool. What is ravishing here is the harmoniousness of the house, and the perfect accord between landscape and habitation, between allegory and domesticity, between the natural world outside and the intimate world of the affections within. All this places Villa Barbaro not only among Palladio's greatest achievements, but among the artistic wonders of northern Italy. Grand, noble, eloquent, personal, and never meretricious, Villa Barbaro remains both civilized and civilizing.

A turning right off the main road, shortly after the handsome Villa Rinaldi, leads to Asolo, a resort village for many a century, as the spacious villas dotted around the hillsides attest. You enter the town through an archway and up narrow arcaded streets to the Piazza Maggiore. Here stands a fine fountain of 1516, its winged lion a more recent addition. The renaissance arcade of Santa Maria di Breda faces on to the piazza. The church, mostly nineteenth-century, houses a grand painting of St Jerome by Sebastiano Bastiani (1488) and a sweetly pious *Assumption*, all cotton-wool clouds and cherubs, by Lorenzo Lotto. Returning to the Piazza Maggiore you'll see on the left the fifteenth-century Loggia del Capitano, now the museum. Its arcades harbour a fresco of the Madonna and Child, and there are sixteenth-century frescoes on the wall facing the piazza. At the top of the square in the corner is the gothic Palazzo Marcello. To the west are the town hall and other houses of remarkable grandeur for so small a town.

The explanation for such grandeur is not mysterious. Caterina Cornaro, the Venetian-born queen of Cyprus, was granted Asolo as a personal fiefdom by way of compensation for her enforced abdication after her husband's suspicious death. The Doge, Agostino Barbarigo, feared that any remarriage on Caterina's part could lead to the loss of Venetian influence over the strategically important island, an outcome that was not to be contemplated. She remained in Asolo for almost twenty years until shortly before her own death in 1510. That she did so in some style is evident from the single surviving element of her palace, the immense broad clock-tower, visible from the Piazza Maggiore. She gathered around her a small court of cultivated noblemen, and one of them, her cousin Cardinal Bembo (1470–1547), recorded some of the dialogues that took place.

Caterina was not the only illustrious resident of Asolo. Robert Browning first visited the town in 1836, when he was a young man. It clearly made a profound impression on him, as forty years later he returned there, and lived for some years at the splendid Villa Pasini. Its broad symmetrical façade, set above terraces, looks down on to Palazzo Marcello from the other side of the square. The celebrated actress Eleonora Duse also bought a house here; the year after her death it was adorned with lines by the poet D'Annunzio, with whom she had been romantically involved. He rather pompously describes her as *apparizione melodiosa*. Duse died in Pittsburgh in 1924, but she had made known her wish to be buried in Asolo, and her bones do indeed lie in the cemetery of Santa Anna.

It is worth making a short detour to the north to visit Possagno. This is the birthplace of the great sculptor Antonio Canova (1757–1822), who was clearly determined that we should never forget it. Above the village is the immense Tempio church, a bizarre marriage of Pantheon and Parthenon. Behind the immense classical portico is a large domed chamber, ninety feet high, its coffered ceiling picked out in white and gold. All this is undeniably impressive if spiritually chilling. The church was Canova's grandiloquent gift to his birthplace. To the right of the choir is a chapel with an altarpiece by Palma Giovane. In another chapel is Canova's bronze *Pietà*, and opposite, the sculptor's tomb and self-portrait of 1812. Canova's heart, never his most convincing attribute, has been removed to the church of the Frari in Venice, where it justifies another

Along Via Caterina at Asolo.

Left **Via Robert Browning at Asolo commemorates one of the town's many famous residents.**

Above **Canova's Tempio at his birthplace, Possagno, an act of homage to classical architecture.**

immense monument to this immodest man. In the village, adjoining the house where he was born, is the museum devoted to his work, mostly in the form of plaster models.

South-west of Possagno is the small town of Crespano, where a *Madonna and Saints* in the parish church is ascribed, implausibly, to Veronese. Head south towards San Zenone and Mussolente and continue westward, passing Antonio Gaidon's splendid Villa Negri Piovene (1763). Steps flanked by hedges climb the steep hill to the tall cream-coloured villa, with its two-storey arcaded pavilions on either side. By continuing a short distance in the same direction, you will soon reach the outskirts of Bassano.

3
Padua and the Euganean Hills

Padua – Arquà Petrarca – Monselice – Este – Praglia

Legend attributes the founding of Padua to the Trojan Antenor in the twelfth century BC. This legend, unsurprisingly, is the invention of an over-fertile imagination, but the town is undoubtedly of ancient origin, and was a settlement of the Veneti people for some centuries before it was transformed into the Roman city of Patavium in 43 BC. Because of its advantageous location along major trade routes, Padua prospered until the Lombards' sacking of the city in 601. In medieval times Padua became a refined centre of learning, and the university that flourishes to this day was founded in 1222, just after the university at Bologna. Padua reaped side benefits from its academic eminence in the form of Italy's first astronomical clock, still in place, and Europe's oldest botanic garden.

By participating in the successful campaigns of the Lombard League against Holy Roman Emperor Frederick Barbarossa, Padua extended its control to other cities such as Bassano and Belluno and Feltre. The usual succession of warlords – Ezzelino III da Romano from 1237 to 1256, then the Scaligeri and the Carraresi – ruled the city. In 1405 the city came under Venetian control, and remained so until the Austrian occupation of 1797. The city walls were constructed in the early sixteenth century in response to the siege by Holy Roman Emperor Maximilian I (1508–19) during the war of the League of Cambrai.

Like all ancient Italian cities, Padua is not a sensible place in which to use a motor car. There are extensive car parks, including a useful long-term car park, in the vast piazza, the largest in Italy, known as Prato della Valle. From here it is only a few minutes' walk to most of the attractions of this richly endowed city. The Prato was once the site of a Roman circus, which explains its oval shape. It was cleaned up in the eighteenth century by the Venetian *podestà*, Andrea Memmi, who established the moated gardens in the centre of the Prato that bear his name, and linked them to the promenades around the square with a series of bridges. Statues, including one by Canova, of prominent Paduans strike dramatic poses along the edges of the park.

The only building of any distinction – other than the plagiaristic charm of the nineteenth-century Venetian-gothic *palazzo* called Loggia Amulea – is the church of Santa Giustina. This massive brick building from the early sixteenth century was built on the site of far more ancient churches erected to commemorate the alleged martyrdom of the saint on this spot. The most striking features of the exterior – the façade remains raw and unfinished – are the eight cupolas, which echo those of the Basilica of San Antonio a short distance away. The architect was Andrea Briosco (1470–1532; also known as Il Riccio), whose more refined work is to be found in

The moated gardens at Prato della Valle in Padua.

the Basilica and other Paduan churches. The interior is a disappointment despite its statistical accomplishment as the largest renaissance church in the Veneto and apparently the eleventh-largest church anywhere. The design is pompous and leaden, a great open space with deep side-chapels and altar-pieces, most of mediocre quality.

Yet Santa Giustina is far from lacking in interest. At the east end is a depiction by Veronese of the saint's martyrdom, and the choir also contains magnificently carved sixteenth-century choir stalls by Riccardo Taurigny, depicting scenes from the Old and New Testaments. Enter the door to the confessionals just south of the choir, and you will find the surviving parts of the older structures. The chapel of St Luke has remnants of good-quality fifteenth-century frescoes by Giovanni Storlato and his followers; these depict the life of the saint and groups of Paduan nobles and bishops. Glass doors, invariably locked, lead into a long corridor, at one end of which is a choir dating

from 1462. (It is worth buttonholing a passing monk to gain access to these parts of the church, as well as to the choir, usually closed to visitors because of repeated vandalism.) This splendid hall contains fine inlaid stalls, the magnificent alabaster tomb slab of Lodovico Barbo (1443), a secular tomb of the same period in a choir recess, and a fine wooden Crucifix.

Return to the main church and the south transept, which contains a sarcophagus of, I am told, relics of St Matthew; the tomb is inlaid with sixteenth-century relief panels. There is an even more impressive sarcophagus in the transept opposite, containing, the monks assure me, the body of St Luke, brought here from Constantinople together with other precious relics. (William Beckford was rightly sceptical, noting these 'altar tombs of very remote antiquity, adorned with uncouth sculptures of the Evangelists'.) This tomb is inlaid with magisterial fourteenth-century Pisan alabaster panels of very fine quality. From the south transept a door leads to a complex of renaissance chapels covered with mediocre frescoes, and the shrine of St Prosdocimo, the first bishop of Padua, which has a very beautiful sixth-century inscribed marble iconostasis.

It is a short walk along the side of the Prato and up Via Belludi to the piazza in front of the Basilica of San Antonio, which every Paduan refers to as Il Santo. The first building on the right is the Museo Civico. The museum is in a state of some confusion, as its contents have either been distributed to other institutions or await relocation in the new municipal museum near the Scrovegni chapel. From the galleries of the museum there is, incidentally, a view on to one of the fine gothic cloisters attached to the Basilica. At the time of writing the museum features a collection of ceramics and furniture, and paintings that include a graceful and fragile fresco of the Madonna and Child by Jacopo da Montagnana, a gilt Crivelli-like *Madonna and Child* by Lazzaro Bastiani (?1425–1512), an incompetent but

The interior of the vast renaissance church of Santa Giustina at Padua.

The Botanic Garden of Padua has been here since the 1550s.

charming *Voyage of the Argonauts* attributed to Lorenzo Costa (1460–1535), and a complex *Adoration of the Magi* by Giovanni Mansueti (d. *c*.1527). The charm of the collection is that these works by little-known painters are often more impressive than works doubtfully attributed to recognised masters. There is also a striking nocturnal *Crucifixion* and a *Last Supper*, both by Veronese. The extensive display of works by the local painter Il Padovanino (Alessandro Varotari; 1598–1648) does not thrill. A seventeenth-century painting entitled *Roman Charity* and attributed to Andrea Celesti shows a greybeard latched onto the breast of a young woman. Charity indeed.

A hall dominated by a vast and astonishingly elaborate fifteenth-century tapestry by Jourdain de

One of the medieval treasures of Padua: the statue of Gattamelata outside the Basilica of San Antonio.

Blaye also contains paintings by Bordone, Tintoretto and Veronese. The next hall displays a hilariously camp military portrait of 1633 by Sebastiano Mazzoni, set within an equally flamboyant frame, and an abundance of tedious eighteenth-century pastoral scenes by the likes of Giuseppe Zais. A side room is devoted to eight panels, recently restored, of questionable quality by Tintoretto; they are thought to be very early works. Finally there are some pretty Longhis and paintings by both Tiepolos.

Next to the museum, Via Orto Botanico leads to one of the city's most precious assets: the botanic garden laid out in the mid 1550s by Andrea Moroni and still preserving its original plan. It still combines a scholarly purpose, for which it was founded, and a purely aesthetic character that soothes its many visitors. Next door to the museum are a number of other ancient buildings. The Scuola del Santo of 1427 contains a stylistically mixed fresco cycle by various sixteenth-century painters, including two early works by Titian of 1511. Most of the panels depict – what doesn't in this part of Padua? – the miracles performed by St Anthony. The whole is greater than the sum of its parts, and the serenity of this chamber is enhanced by the very beautiful coffered ceiling, and the polychrome terracotta statue of the Madonna and Child (1520) by Andrea Briosco. Adjoining the Scuola is the Oratorio di San Giorgio, frescoed by Altichiero (*c*.1330–95), but for some time it has been closed to visitors.

Opposite these buildings rises the equestrian statue of Gattamelata, a Venetian *condottiere* whose real name was Erasmo da Narni, and whose tomb rests in a south aisle chapel of the basilica. This great statue by the Florentine Donatello was the first major bronze to be cast in Italy and is thus of the greatest artistic importance. Donatello was born, it is thought, in 1386, and lived for eighty years. In his native Florence he worked with Ghiberti. His early works, notably his wood carvings, are essentially gothic in style, despite their striking individuality. By the time he was lured to Padua in 1443 he was an artist of renown. He must have known from the outset that the commission

Exuberant stonework on the Teatro Ridotto in Padua.

would be a controversial one, for this was the first time that an equestrian statue would commemorate someone who was not a member of a ruling house. It was to take ten years before the statue was placed on its plinth outside the basilica. Visible from most approaches, the statue occupies a dramatic position, but unfortunately its height makes it difficult to see the details of the design.

The basilica itself is enfolded within a brick exterior that gives some hint of the exotic splendours within. The west façade is enlivened by white marble arches and a rhythmic loggia topped by a frivolous little minaret, but the most striking external feature, best seen from the side and rear, is the opulent confusion of domes and arcades, campaniles and conical roofs. There are echoes of San Marco in Venice, but there are also countless other echoes, as elements of byzantine, gothic, and quasi-Moorish design all find expression in this remarkable composition. Most thirteenth-century

churches in the Veneto have dull brick exteriors, but there is nothing dull about Il Santo. Although its jumble of disparate elements appears confused, the composition is almost perfectly symmetrical.

The church was begun in 1232 to memorialize the famous saint who died the previous year and is buried within. Anthony was a native of Lisbon, having been born there in 1195. Only in 1221 did he leave Portugal, to take up a number of academic appointments at French and Italian universities. In 1230 he abandoned formal theology for the pleasures of preaching, notably against usury and avarice. These are not accomplishments usually rewarded by canonization, but Anthony had other gifts, and was regarded as a miracle worker by many of his followers. Since his canonization in 1232 his brief as a saint has become more broadly based: he is regarded as the patron of the poor, and is supposedly adept in arranging the return of lost property to its owners. His benevolent powers can also be invoked by travellers and pregnant women, and by those in desperate straits. No wonder he is popular.

Il Santo was not completed until a century later. And it shows, since the nave is composed of hefty gothic piers encrusted with monuments, while the choir is a more sophisticated high-gothic performance. If the nave and aisles lack elegance, that is because the primary function of the arcades is to support the series of domes over the main axis of the church. The gothic and byzantine austerity of the nave gives way to the livelier rhythms of the choir, with its radiating chapels and ambulatory.

Begin by looking at the south chapels. Starting from the west end, the fifth chapel, that of San Felice, is covered with late fourteenth-century frescoes by Altichiero and his contemporary, Jacopo Avanzo. On either side of an overcrowded Crucifixion scene spread over three panels are scenes from the life of St James. Although time has dulled some of the colours and fuzzed the clarity of line, this remains a superb cycle,

The exotic domes and steeples of the basilica of Il Santo in Padua.

so beautifully contained within the broad chapel, complete with tombs and stalls and, on the superstructure separating chapel from nave, a row of statues by Andreolo de' Santi, who designed the chapel. In his gift for narrative and varied use of colour, Altichiero clearly shows the influence of Giotto (1266/7−1337), with whose work in Padua the younger painter must surely have been thoroughly familiar.

Just beyond the chapel, a door leads into one of the four cloisters of the basilica. The passageway is lined with tombs, three of them frescoed beneath their canopies. More tombs and plaques, many medieval, line the walls of this fine airy gothic cloister. One of them memorializes Thomas Howard, who collected the Arundel marbles and who died in 1646. Return to the church and the entrance to the ambulatory. Pass with haste or admiration, according to taste, the chapel adorned with meretricious frescoes by Pietro Annigoni (1910−88). The dimly lit choir chapels are mostly without interest; for the most part, their frescoes are modern pastiche. The east chapel, however, the Chapel of the Relics, is hard to ignore. This is a monstrous example of late baroque exuberance, especially the decorations of the cupola; but the sixteenth-century statues by Bernini's pupil Filippo Parodi are of good quality. Within the chapel, glass cases display dozens of medieval reliquaries, and within them repose the kind of fragments that Chaucer referred to as 'pigges bones'. The casket from which the bones of St Anthony were disinterred, and his habit, are also on display.

Continue past the north ambulatory chapels to the small group of chapels on the right. The east chapel, one of the few remnants of the earlier church, displays a medieval gilt statue of the Black Madonna, though there is nothing black about it. Note too the fine marble wall tomb with its equestrian portrait. The adjoining Cappella dei Conti is embellished with a ravishing fresco cycle of 1382 by the Florentine artist Giusto de' Menabuoi. It's arguable that the frescoes have been over-restored, but at least they are clear and legible, a vivid and imaginative depiction of scenes from the lives of Blessed Luca Velludi, who is buried in the chapel, and of St James and St Philip. The large panel to the left of the altar includes a precious and wonderfully detailed cityscape of medieval Padua.

The next chapel to the west could hardly be in greater contrast. Built to designs by Andrea Briosco, it forms a renaissance counterpart to the gothic San Felice chapel directly opposite. Briosco's design, which also has an elaborate marble superstructure, is cool and elegant and celebratory rather than devotional. Cleverly carved arcades enclose high reliefs depicting the life of St Anthony. The reliefs date from the early sixteenth century and are the work of, among others, Sansovino and Tullio Lombardo, who signed his two panels. Although many of the groups are excessively composed, with every flamboyant gesture made in seeming isolation, the overall effect, given unity by the false perspective employed in all the panels, is stunning. Devotion has its place among all this display, and supplicants have attached to the tomb colour photographs of loved ones in trouble, as well as photographs of wrecked cars that will look familiar to foreign motorists in Italy. This is nothing new. Joseph Addison, writing his *Remarks on Italy* at the very end of the seventeenth century, noted that among the votaries in this chapel were 'wretched daubings, impertinent inscriptions, hands, legs, and arms of wax, with a thousand idle offerings of the same nature'. The next chapel contains an elaborate but cold funerary monument by Pietro Lombardo, and this aisle also grants space to a few grandiloquent baroque monuments that climb the walls.

Return to the crossing and the high altar. The marble altar rail is decorated with four sinuous bronzes (1593) by Tiziano Aspetti, but the bronze statues and reliefs and Crucifix on the high altar itself are far more arresting. The work of Donatello and his followers, they date from 1446 to 1450. Donatello had come to Padua in 1443 to work on the Gattamelata statue, but his contributions to the altar of Il Santo constitute an

Fourteenth-century frescoes by Altichiero adorn the chapel of San Felice in Il Santo.

Exotic street furniture in Padua: a lamppost in Piazza del Santo.

equally great achievement. Moreover, he founded in the process a school of followers, who contributed abundantly to the city. Persuade the sacristans to allow you into the choir, as these masterpieces must be examined close up, as must the bronze reliefs depicting Old Testament scenes on either side of the sanctuary. These are by Bartolomeo Bellano and Andrea Briosco and are wonderfully detailed – consummate artistry indeed. The *Deposition* inserted into the back of the altar seems overblown and coarse in comparison, but the reliefs on the high altar are of impeccable quality. Of the great statues above the altar, the *Virgin Enthroned* stands out as an especially complex and forceful expression of this familiar theme.

Returning down the nave, note the medieval frescoes of the Virgin Mary behind the pulpit and on the next pier on the left. The following pier bears Sammicheli's monument to Cardinal Bembo, who died in 1547, and whose name is revered by all typophiles.

He was the author of the dialogue *De Aetna*, published by Aldus Manutius in Venice in 1495; the typeface used by Aldus was recut in 1929 and named after Bembo, and acquired an immediate popularity that persists to this day.

The *Martyrdom of St Agatha* on the far side of this pier is by G. B. Tiepolo, an incongruous contribution to these surroundings. Moving from the west end back to the altar, the second pier on the left is enveloped by the Contarini monument (1558), a vulgar piece of bombast by Alessandro Vittoria and Sammicheli, in lamentable contrast to the simple refinement of the Bembo monument opposite, and to the contemporaneous Girolamo Michiel monument two piers to the east.

On leaving Il Santo walk behind the basilica into Via Cesarotti, past the pilgrims' hostel. Close by, within the precincts of the basilica, are Giovanni Maria Falconetto's elegant Loggia Cornara (1524) and the Odeum (completed in 1542) but unfortunately they have been closed to the public for some time. They were both commissioned by the humanist patron of the arts Alvise Cornaro, who used the Loggia for theatrical performances and the Odeum for musical performances. Cornaro was more than a rich dilettante; he contributed substantially to the reclamation of delta land along the Adriatic coast. These days he is better remembered for his treatise on architecture than for his writings on the Stoic philosophers. In the treatise he dealt not only with the essential elements of design and proportion, but with more peripheral matters such as furnishings and lavatory design. It seems probable that Palladio made the acquaintance of Cornaro in the late 1530s, and features of Falconetto's buildings and reflections of Cornaro's published theories crop up in some of Palladio's early sketches. These works by Falconetto (1468–1535), with their punctilious imitation of the classical orders, are important precursors of the style later brought to perfection by Palladio.

Medieval arcades along Via San Francesco in Padua offer shelter from both sun and rain.

Turn left up Via San Francesco. On the left you will see the broad arcades alongside the sixteenth-century church of San Francesco. One of the south chapels is frescoed, work attributed to Girolamo de' Santo, and on either side of the choir are renaissance tombs, and two large bronze reliefs up on the east walls. These are two portions of the monument to Dottore Roccabonella (1498) by Bellano and Briosco, the same team responsible for the reliefs in the basilica choir. From the sacristy a door leads into the simple cloister with its pleasantly unkempt garden.

Follow the lane opposite San Francesco, Via Santa Sofia, to the medieval church of that name. One of the oldest medieval structures in Padua, Santa Sofia has an elegant brick façade of rising blind arcades. The rib-vaulted interior is plain but exceptionally lovely, with a complex articulation of aisle arcades and beautifully carved capitals. Behind the deep plump choir is a narrow ambulatory, screened by an arcade of columns with only partially completed carved capitals. In the north aisle is a late medieval polychrome *Pietà*. Leave by the north aisle door to look at the apse exterior, a complex composition of arcades and galleries showing both Roman and byzantine influences. Next to the church is a fine *palazzo* by Scamozzi.

Return to Via San Francesco and continue up it, passing at no. 27 the imposing but graceless Palazzo Zabarella, with its blunt corner tower and battlements and renaissance fenestration. The palaces at nos. 11 and 9 have been heavily restored and altered, but a plaque on no. 9, Palazzo Romanin-Jacur, assures us that Dante was here in 1306. Across the road is the Antenor monument (1233), a massive sarcophagus beneath a brick baldacchino and the supposed tomb of the Trojan warrior, but in reality the repository of the bones of a tenth-century Hungarian soldier. Joseph Addison observed loftily three centuries ago: 'What they here show for the ashes of Livy and Antenor is disregarded by the best of their own antiquaries.' In

the unlikely setting of the pedestrian subway a few yards further along you will find a well preserved Roman bridge.

The next block brings us to the university. No. 3, Palazzo Capodivacca, with its elegant renaissance windows, has been incorporated into the more brutish modern buildings. The university is known locally as Il Bo', (the Ox), named after the inn that once stood on this site. The university attained great importance since in medieval times there was no other such institution close to Venice. Turn right into Via VIII Febbraio, a welcome pedestrian precinct that traverses the heart of Padua; here you will see the principal façade of the university, dating from the eighteenth century. Enter Moroni's courtyard of 1552, with its severe double loggia, crammed with frescoes and cartouches with armorial bearings. The historic halls on the first floor have been closed for restoration since June 1989. I did visit them – thanks to the helpfulness of a custodian of sly humour who insisted I should only talk Italian in Italy when I thought I was doing exactly that – and I could see no restoration work in progress.

The Aula Magna, used for university ceremonies, is a fine chamber, its walls filled with coats of arms and plaques. In an adjoining room stands the rickety pulpit from which Galileo (1546–1642) delivered his lectures. The medical hall displays in a glass case the skulls of eight former professors of medicine. Padua University, indeed, was best known for its medical faculty: the great Vesalius (1514–64) taught here, and William Harvey (1578–1657) and John Caius (1510–73) studied here, as did Oliver Goldsmith (1730–74) some time later. The future kings of Sweden and Hungary also put in appearances. Nonetheless, an observer writing in 1687, Gilbert Burnet, was none too impressed, reporting: 'There are no men of any great fame now in it; and the quarrels among the students have driven away most of the strangers that used to come and study here; for it is not safe to stir abroad here after sunset.'

The anatomical theatre of 1594, designed by Fabrizio d'Acquapendente, is one of the oldest in Europe (Pisa's is said to date from 1552) and was in use until

The renaissance courtyard of the ancient university at Padua.

1872. A chamber beneath this wooden bowl of a theatre allowed the corpse to be wheeled in and hoisted up to the ground floor. Next to it sat the professor in the only comfortable chair in the hall, while the students perched around, bat-like, on six levels, leaning over the finely pierced balustrades. A surprisingly small and fragile wooden structure, like an old galleon, the steep little theatre served its primary function of permitting an intense concentration on the flayed object below. Goethe, in 1786, was less impressed: 'In spite of all its fame, the university shocked me. I am glad I did not have to study there. Such a cramped school is unimaginable even to a German student, who often suffered agonies on the hard benches of the auditorium. The anatomical theatre, in particular, is an example of how to squeeze as many students together as possible.'

On emerging into Via VIII Febbraio turn right and you will soon come to Japelli's neo-classical Café Pedrocchi. Completed in 1831, the café played a role in 1848 as a gathering place for insurrectionists against the Austrian occupation. Despite, or perhaps because of, the gracious surroundings, the revolt failed. The design seems poor on paper: the porticoes seem squat and dumpy, with thick columns and heavy entablatures, but the conception works beautifully, and subtly combines an elegant interior with a sense of accessibility, as glass doors at either end allow patrons to walk right through the café. In the nineteenth century it never closed. Upstairs are a number of exquisitely decorated rooms, once used for meetings and conspiracies, now used for exhibitions. There is an octagonal Greek room, an Etruscan room, and a circular Roman room, all named for their decorative schemes. A very pretty renaissance room is painted blue and gold, the Herculaneum room is exceptionally fey, and the ballroom is appropriately dedicated to Rossini (1792–1868). He would have appreciated the gossamer lightness of the fourteen white stucco figures leaping from high on the walls and holding laurel wreaths aloft. Most dramatic of all is the Egyptian room, painted an uncompromising black and midnight blue. All this is thoroughly frivolous, but this makes it all the more welcome in a city filled with masterpieces of art and architecture.

Continue up the street towards two of the squares with which this part of Padua is dotted: Cavour and Garibaldi. On the way you'll pass the Caffè Cavour, where I regularly bought some of the richest and most satisfying pastries in town. At Piazza Garibaldi you'll see on the right the Altinate Gate, part of the thirteenth-century fortifications. By turning right down Via Altinate, which contains many fine gothic *palazzi*, you will reach Scamozzi's church of San Gaetano (1586), which is enlivened by the use of coloured marbles and by the dashing if ill-proportioned statues in the niches between the pilasters. Return to Piazza Garibaldi and go up Corso Garibaldi and take the first right, which brings you to the long brick church of the Eremitani. Bear left and enter the gate leading to the Capella Scrovegni and the new Museo Civico. The chapel can only accommodate about sixty visitors (or five hundred schoolchildren) at any one time, so try to visit it outside peak periods to avoid a long wait. The brick chapel, consisting of a plain barrel-vaulted nave and a short rib-vaulted choir, was built in 1303 by Enrico Scrovegni. Scrovegni was an extremely rich man, but his honour was somewhat tainted by the fact that a large part of these riches, which he inherited, was derived by his father from usury, a failing for which Dante consigned him to one of the circles of Hell. Enrico commissioned Giotto to decorate the interior, and the artist provided thirty-eight panels depicting the life of Jesus. Every other inch of the nave was painted too, mostly by Giotto's pupils. The two walls are arched over by a vault painted deep blue with gold stars, and into this firmament are set medallions, the work of Giotto's assistants. On the west wall is a complex depiction of the Last Judgment. On the altar stand three marble statues by Giovanni Pisano (1245–1320), including an exquisite Madonna and Child, and on the wall behind the altar is the refined tomb of Scrovegni himself, designed by Andreolo de' Santi.

Giotto's cycle seems quintessentially medieval in conception, despite the claims made for the artist's sophistication and modernity or humanism. What Giotto does bring to these familiar tableaux is luminosity, grace, an impeccable sense of composition and colour, and perfect clarity. Nor should one disparage the sheer prettiness of the frescoes: their delicate pastel colours, the deep blue skies, the white and pink marble of the architectural backgrounds. The frescoes are, in their way, perfect: lovingly composed, pure in feeling, and very beautiful. *The Flight into Egypt*, for instance, is just one of many flawless panels. Art historians laud the psychological realism of Giotto, but I do not find it. There is something almost bland about the sheer perfection of the painting. Even the panel of the *Crucifixion* is hardly imbued with deep spiritual feeling. The *Resurrection* too lacks drama. Just recall what Piero della Francesca (1416–92) made of that climactic moment. Of course it is unfair to compare two masters of very different ages, and Giotto in comparison with his contemporaries is evidently a towering figure. No visitor to the Veneto should miss the Scrovegni chapel, but neither should visitors, here or anywhere else, be totally cowed by received opinion, including this one.

The Palazzo Scrovegni, which the chapel adjoined, no longer exists. What does remain, and is visible on leaving the chapel, is part of the Roman amphitheatre that once stood here. Within the gardens, in some of the monastic buildings of the Eremitani, the new Museo Civico is housed. The lower galleries contain extensive archaeological and lapidary collections, notably the tomb of the Roman Volumni family, and fine mosaic floors and a small Egyptian section. Upstairs are renaissance bronzes, including some by Briosco and his workshop, and the Museo Battacin, a collection of nineteenth-century Italian art, most of it awash in sentimentality. The large collection of paintings includes two tiny and modest panels by Giorgione, a portrait by Giovanni Bellini, and panels by Michele Giambono (*fl.*1420–62), Lorenzo Veneziano (*fl.*1356–72), and Guariento di Arpo (1338–68/70), and the almost voluptuous *Crucifixion* by Giotto that originally hung in the Scrovegni chapel.

Return to the Eremitani. This gaunt structure used

The virile statue of Petrarch in the Paduan piazza that bears his name.

to be one of the great artistic sites in Europe, until a bombing raid in 1944 wrecked the church. The structure was rebuilt after the war, but it was impossible to replace the glorious frescoes by Andrea Mantegna, of which only fragments remain. Enter the church through the renaissance south portal. The wooden roof, also reconstructed, is a remarkable piece of carpentry that runs the length of the church. Facing each other along the walls at the west end are two vast fourteenth-century monuments to members of the Carrara family, which ruled Padua from 1318 to 1405. The north choir chapel contains a more modest late fourteenth-century monument to Ilario Sanguinacci, whose armoured effigy lies atop the sarcophagus, and faded traces of frescoes (1370) by Giusto de' Menabuoi. On the altar reposes a fifteenth-century polychrome *Madonna and Child*. A fine painted Crucifix from the fourteenth century dominates the choir.

The large chapel south of the choir is the Cappella

Ovetari. It can only be entered with anguish, as its walls have only traces of Mantegna's fresco cycle. Andrea Mantegna was born near Padua in 1431, so he must have been familiar with the magnificent frescoes by Giotto and Menabuoi and others that we are still enjoying today. He obviously absorbed the visual lessons they offered very rapidly, since the Ovetari frescoes exhibit extraordinary maturity. They date from 1448 to 1456, when Mantegna was still a very young man (he lived until 1506), yet even then he was in possession of an essentially renaissance sensibility. Colour, gesture, psychological acuity, command over not only perspective but space too – all were achieved with astonishing mastery and sureness of touch. The loss of these frescoes is incalculable.

On emerging from the church, head north on Corso Garibaldi, then left on Via Giotto and left again on Via del Carmine, which brings you to the church of that name. It's a strange-looking gothic structure with a partly marble-faced façade, deep side bays beneath a cornice, and a green-roofed dome over the crossing. The central portal has impressive wooden doors. The dull interior, remodelled in the sixteenth century, is redeemed by a high altar of white and lilac marble. There is more interesting matter next door in the adjoining Scuoletta del Carmine of 1377, which has a cycle of frescoes by Domenico (c.1484–c.1563) and Giulio Campagnola (c.1482–after 1514). Unfortunately the sacristan regards it as an affront if you ask to see them, but you may have better luck than I did.

With the church behind you, walk down towards the Ponte Molino and the gateway just beyond it, the sole survivor of the fourteen gates built by the Carraresi in the fourteenth century, and continue down Via Dante, which is lined with many fine gothic and renaissance *palazzi*. When you come to Corso Milano, you will see on the right the curved lines of Japelli's nineteenth-century Teatro Verdi. Cross the Corso and take the first right, which leads to the small church of San Nicolò. Although of romanesque origin, it has been much tampered with, yet remains attractive. There are fragmentary frescoes in the north aisle, a late medieval triptych in a south chapel, and an altar-piece by G. D. Tiepolo (1727–1804). Return to Via Dante, turn right, then left into Via Santa Lucia, a lane filled with sombre gothic houses.

This leads to the church of Santa Lucia, of interest only for the lively series of statues by Giovanni Bonazza (*fl.*1695–1730) set in niches around the interior. At right angles to the church is the two-storey Oratorio (or Scuola) di San Rocco, adorned with frescoes depicting the life of that saint by many hands, including Domenico Campagnola and Gualtieri. In parlous condition, the frescoes have been undergoing careful restoration for years. Although highly regarded, only two or three of the panels seem of exciting quality.

Continue down Via Santa Lucia, passing on the right some of the oldest *palazzi* in Padua. You will emerge into Piazza Garibaldi. Turn right into the pedestrian precinct, and after Café Pedrocchi turn right into the 1930s façade of the town hall complex. A broad flight of steps leads past a courtyard by Moroni and up into the Salone, the astonishing hall of the Palazzo della Ragione. Originally built in 1219 as Padua was struggling to establish its independent identity, the Salone was altered in 1306 by Giovanni degli Eremiti. The vast space, 79 m long and 26 m high, is spanned by a simple keel roof, most recently reconstructed in the 1750s. It was Giovanni who raised the height of the walls and knocked down partitions to form the huge space we see today. The walls were once filled with frescoes by Giotto, but they were destroyed in a fire of 1426, and have been replaced by lively but mostly routine frescoes by Niccolò Miretto (*fl.*1430) and others, depicting matters religious, secular, and astronomical. William Beckford, in 1780, was quite overwhelmed by the Salone: 'The roof, one spacious vault of brown timber, casts a solemn gloom, which was still increased by the lateness of the hour, and not diminished by the wan light, admitted through the windows of pale blue glass. The size and shape of this colossal chamber . . . and, above all, the watery gleams that glanced through the dull casements, possessed my fancy with Noah's ark, and almost persuaded me I beheld that extraordinary vessel.'

Succulent white asparagus: one of the Veneto's many local specialities.

The Salone, often used for exhibitions, permanently houses an immense wooden horse, a magnified copy dating from 1466 of Donatello's Gattamelata statue that was used during tournaments. On either side of the Salone a loggia on two storeys overlooks Piazza della Frutta to the north and Piazza delle Erbe to the south. Both the squares and the ground floor of the Palazzo are still used for markets. These Italian markets – their equivalents can be found in most towns of any size – are quite remarkable, both for their abundance and their variety. I love the colours of the ranks of multicoloured peppers and scarlet tomatoes and glowering artichokes. At the right time of year you can choose from three or four different varieties of asparagus, and there is always a good choice of lettuces and greenery.

Descend into Piazza delle Frutta, from where there is a clear view of this extraordinary medieval building and its loggias. Between the Palazzo della Ragione and the tall thirteenth-century tower of the Palazzo del Podestà, now incorporated into the town hall, is the Palazzo del Consiglio of 1238, supported on columns with two byzantine capitals. At the far end of the square Via San Clemente leads into another square, the spacious Piazza dei Signori; at the far end is the early seventeenth-century Palazzo del Capitanio, a former seat of municipal government. It incorporates in its tower an astronomical clock by Giovanni Dondi that dates from 1344, making it the oldest in Italy. The elegant white renaissance building with a ground floor loggia, located on the south side of the square, is the Gran Guardia, completed in 1523. All these piazzas – and there are almost a dozen of them in central Padua – allow the city and its visitors to breathe and stretch, so it is all the more difficult to recognize a description that a seventeenth-century traveller, William Lithgow, gave of the city as 'the most melancholy city of Europe, the cause only arising of the narrow passage of the open streets, and of the long galleries, and dark ranges of pillars, that go all where on every hand of you through the whole streets of the town'. Lithgow was also alarmed by the high incidence of murder and sodomy, and was clearly of an anxious disposition.

Walk beneath the clock-tower and Falconetto's sumptuous archway, and you find yourself in yet another square, Corte Capitaniato, now part of the university. Enter the courtyard in the far left corner and mount the long flight of steps that leads to the Sala dei Giganti, now used as a concert hall. This immense room appears even more capacious beneath its fine coffered ceiling. The two short walls, west and east, are punched through with large windows, but every other surface is covered with sixteenth-century frescoes of classical heroes by Domenico Campagnola and others. They're not very good, as most of the artists couldn't draw, but they are suitably pompous for the location. The Sala is a surviving section of the Carraresi palace that once stood here.

On descending the staircase turn right, and pass under the arch into the Piazza del Duomo. The cathedral was built by Andrea da Valle and Agostino Righetti in 1552, and they loosely modelled the apse on a design by Michelangelo. Of greater interest is the romanesque baptistery, rebuilt in 1260. This stylishly proportioned brick building is topped by a cupola-supporting drum, ornamented, like the rest of the baptistery, with blind arcading. The Florentine artist Menabuoi was commissioned by the wife of Francesco I da Carrara to paint the frescoes within, and completed them in about 1380. The cycle lacks the schematic clarity of that in the Cappella Scrovegni, and, like Altichiero and other contemporary artists, Menabuoi liked to cram as much as possible into the vast surface at his disposal. This cycle is less imaginative, less bold in conception, than the one he contributed to the Cappella dei Conti in Il Santo. There is something dogged about it ('only twenty more saints to go . . .'), but nonetheless this is a major achievement. The *Annunciation* and *Baptism of Christ*, for example, are beautifully composed, and more than make up for the sloppiness of, say, the *Slaughter of the Innocents*. In the centre of the dome is a formidable half-figure of Christ encircled by saints and angels. The very beautiful polyptych on the altar is also by Menabuoi. Note too the substantial thirteenth-century font with its twisted half-pillars.

Like Santa Giustina, the cathedral is a building without warmth, though it is far more stylish. Two curious features of the interior are the combination of domes and barrel-vaulting in the nave and crossing, and the depth of the transepts. In the north transept is the finely carved gothic monument to Bishop Paleo da Prata with a sloping effigy; and in the other transept is the monument, grander but less refined than Prata's, to Cardinal Zabarella (1427). The sacristy contains a fine collection of paintings, church treasures, and illuminated manuscripts, but they may be viewed only with special permission. Emerging from the *duomo*, you can enjoy its tranquil piazza from one of the cafés opposite. On one side of the square is the bishop's palace, on the other Falconetto's stylish renaissance façade of the Monte di Pietà.

On the far side of the piazza, next to the old pharmacy, Via Manin leads into Piazza delle Erbe, with its spectacular market with the Palazzo della Ragione as an even more spectacular backdrop. Walk through the piazza, turning right into the pedestrian precinct and passing the university until you come to the hall-like church of Santa Maria dei Servi. It dates from the late fourteenth century, although the arcades facing the street on the east side date from 1510 and are composed of reused capitals from Il Santo supported on very slender columns. The interior is unappealing, and dominated by the gigantic and utterly tasteless rococo altar-piece by Giovanni Bonazza on the west wall. This also overshadows the few frescoes in the church, though they are too faded to give much pleasure, with the singular exception of a small poignant *Pietà* by Jacopo da Montagnana to the right of the rococo horror.

On leaving the church, turn right and continue straight into Via Umberto. On the right you will immediately see the battered but beautiful buff-coloured Casa Olzignani of 1466. Its fenestration shows a curious blend of Venetian-gothic and renaissance styles. (If you fancy a stroll with no other purpose than to enjoy the quiet streets where Paduans actually live, turn right down Via dei Rogati, with its many old houses and *palazzi*. You will reach the Barbarigo bridge, and can then follow the river bank, returning to Prato delle Valle through the back streets. The large tower on the other side of the river, the Specola, is a remnant of the medieval fortifications, and was converted into the city observatory two centuries ago.) Back on Via Umberto, no. 82, marked by its tall brick tower, is the massive thirteenth-century Palazzo Capodilista. The street opens into Prato della Valle.

South of Padua lie the gentle Colli Euganei, the peculiarly conical Euganean hills, which have been a resort area since Roman times. From Padua follow signs for Abano Terme, a spa celebrated for two thousand years for its mud cures. At the entrance to the town from the north is San Lorenzo, which has a fine romanesque campanile with blind arcading and a

The conical hills and undulating valleys of the volcanic Colli Euganei near Teolo.

conical roof. Two kilometres away are the major thermal springs and hotels, large blocks set among gardens. The very fact that these spas are devoted to therapeutic purposes makes me imagine them essentially unhealthy places, guaranteed to make any ailment worse. My fears are evidently not shared by the thousands of visitors, Germans as well as Italians, who come here to be smeared with mud and immersed in pools under the watchful eye of burly nurses.

Merging into Abano from the south is Montegrotto Terme. Between its railway station and the town centre, near the Hotel Montecarlo, are some large Roman excavations: a theatre and baths are among the discoveries here. Adjoining the two spas is the village of Monteortone, where, set against the hillside, is the Sanctuary of Madonna della Salute. Its slender campanile has an elegant witch's-cap roof, and the west door is robustly carved. The sacristy contains frescoes by Jacopo da Montagnana. Nearby is the village of Tramonte, with the lush eighteenth-century Villa delle Rose.

Continue south-west towards Torreglia. Just north of this village is Luvigliano, overlooked by the early sixteenth-century Villa dei Vescovi, which has been attributed to Falconetto, though there is much evidence to suggest that Alvise Cornaro, the patron of both Falconetto and the young Palladio, had a hand in the design. Flights of steps sweep up to a terrace and then to a huge arcaded loggia around three sides of the house, a design that is grand but pretentious. Falconetto's incorporation of the loggia as a dominant feature of the villa anticipates Palladio's own preoccupation with the relation between architecture and landscape. Standing at the gates, I stared up towards the house, and a woman, whether chatelaine or maid I could not tell, came rushing out on to the terrace and yelled down at me, asking me what I wanted. I replied with what I hoped was the Italian equivalent of 'Just looking', but she continued to yell at me until she tired of the sport and retreated indoors.

A hilltop farm near Torreglia in the Colli Euganei.

South-west of Torreglia the sixteenth-century monastery of Eremo di Rua fills a hilltop site. Although the monastery itself is closed to visitors, the views from here over the volcanic Colli Euganei are hard to beat. Continue south-east through yet another spa, Galzignano Terme, then south to Valsanzibio, where the grounds of Villa Barbarigo are open to the public. The eighteenth-century villa is a neat, lofty house, with a raised pedimented central bay, but it is of marginal interest compared to the magnificence of the baroque gardens, filled with fountains and lakes, statues, parterres, and fine trees. Planned by Antonio Barbarigo in 1669, these are undoubtedly among the great gardens of the Veneto, even though many of the magnificent cypress avenues were destroyed during World War II. After seeing Barbarigo it is curious to read Joseph Addison's complaint in *Remarks on Italy*: 'I have not yet seen any gardens in Italy worth taking notice of.'

Head south to Arquà Petrarca, a charming village enfolded within the hills; it justifiably appropriated the name of the great poet who spent his last years here. Indeed, Petrarch's sarcophagus, inscribed with the epitaph he composed for himself, stands in the main square. In 1630 a Dominican monk from Portogruaro broke a corner of the tomb and snatched the skeletal arm of the poet. Exactly why he went to such trouble never became clear. Behind the tomb the romanesque church, though much restored, is well worth a visit. In the choir is an *Assumption* by Palma Giovane and the nave walls are decorated with fragmentary frescoes. Those opposite the north door are byzantine and probably date from the twelfth century, and next to them is a polyptych of St Augustine flanked by other saints. The frescoes on the north wall are probably fifteenth-century.

Arquà Petrarca is a village for strolling through at leisure, for it is filled with ancient houses and renaissance villas. At the top of the village is Petrarch's own, quite substantial, house, with some interesting furnishings and relics, such as the poet's chair. Although the house has been considerably altered over the centuries and the loggia was added in the sixteenth century, the view from here on to the hills can hardly have changed since Petrarch's time. This was not sufficient to impress Mrs Trollope, who visited Arquà in the 1840s and described it as 'a miserable-looking village', adding: 'How any honest man in his senses can ever have thought that "Arqua is delightfully situated" I am at a loss to conceive ... Nor is [Petrarch's] house indicative of much more splendour than the garden.' She found it small and unimpressive, and could discern none of the charm and tranquillity that later visitors have relished.

There is something infinitely touching about the fact that Petrarch chose to end his span of seventy years (1304–74) in this village, for he was the most cosmopolitan of poets. His family having been exiled from Florence, he spent his childhood in Pisa and Carpentras, and studied at Montpellier and Bologna. He travelled widely but returned constantly to another secluded village, to his house at Vaucluse. He spent many years in Rome, and eight years at the Visconti court in Milan, then another few years at Venice, where he was lent a house by the Senate. Can one imagine such civic honour for a poet in Europe today? After a spell at another court, that of Francesco da Carrara at Padua, he retired to Arquà with his illegitimate daughter Francesca, who had been born in 1343. As his creative life slowly ebbed during the last years of his life, he must have been consoled by the knowledge that he was one of the great European masters of literature: capable of composing Latin epics as well as tender lyrics and complex allegories in the vernacular, a polemicist and religious contemplative as well as a major poet.

Just below Petrarch's house is the Oratorio della Trinità, a chapel of romanesque origin, with mutilated frescoes and another altar-piece by Palma Giovane.

From Arqua take the road to Monselice, a small town the Romans named *mons silicis* after the trachyte deposits in the hills around the town, which succeeding generations have ruthlessly extracted and carted off to Venice and other cities as building material. My own first visit to Monselice took place at a time when the southern Veneto was blanketed in a fog

that remained motionless for over a week, keeping Verona's airport closed for days. Driving into Monselice at night at a snail's pace, I stopped the car to ask a man standing at the entrance to his house where I could find the local hotel. 'There,' he said, pointing straight ahead into the dark grey swirl. I could see nothing, and he explained that the hotel was a mere twenty metres away on the other side of a brook. Crossing the narrow bridge that led towards the hotel, I passed the neon sign of a pizzeria that, as I discovered on many subsequent occasions, also cooked up some of the tastiest shellfish south of Padua.

Monselice was variously occupied by great medieval families, notably the Carraresi, who began their rule in 1337, and came under lasting Venetian domination in 1405. After the war of the League of Cambrai in the early sixteenth century, Monselice, like the other fortified towns encircling Padua, lost its defensive function, and the walls and towers fell into a state of disrepair. Opposite the tourist office in the main square, the Piazza Mazzini, you can see some of the remaining town fortifications and the Torre Civica, built by Ezzelino III da Romano in 1244. From the square the Via del Santuario leads up to the main sights of the town. After a few paces you come to the castle, Ca' Marcello, a formidable complex of buildings. The massive tower with stone armoreal bearings is known as Ezzelino's tower, and contains the armoury. Here are displayed weapons of most inventive ferocity, of which my favourite is a crucifix concealing a stiletto, used for bestowing eternal life and the *coup de grâce* simultaneously. Upstairs is a series of public rooms, one with a delightful coffered ceiling, each panel painted with a different bird or animal. Tapestries and superb furniture, the personal collection of the Cini family and one of the finest in all Italy, fill the castle. In one of the bedrooms stands a most beautiful wooden medieval Madonna from Aosta, and the castle also contains a sexy fourteenth-century Pisan Madonna of

Some of the most splendid baroque gardens in Italy are found at Villa Barbarigo near Valsanzibio.

Above **The great medieval poet Petrarch lived close to this ancient oratory in Arquà Petrarca.**

Right **Inside the baroque gardens at Villa Nani-Mocenigo in Monselice.**

The elegant porch of the *duomo* at Monselice.

white marble. Other rooms sport superb fireplaces, notably the Camino Carraresi of 1340, with its four tiers of crude painted trefoiled arcades, like a papal tiara. The remarkably well-equipped medieval kitchen in the basement makes a fascinating conclusion to the visit.

Further up the Via Santuario you'll see, alongside the Villa Nani-Mocenigo, a baroque flight of steps rushing up the hillside to a pavilion. Positioned on the wall on either side of the villa are eighteenth-century stone figures of dwarves (*nani*). Straight ahead is the *duomo*, a finely proportioned thirteenth-century hall church with a fifteenth-century Venetian polyptych on the altar and traces of older frescoes on the choir walls. Behind the *duomo* is the robust romanesque campanile, and a terrace overlooking modern Monselice, which boasts one of the ugliest modern cathedrals in Europe. At the very top of the lane is Villa Duodo, now part of Padua University. Seven chapels mark the ascent for pilgrims; these, and the decorative but uninspired villa, are by Scamozzi. The pilgrims are

coming not to the villa but to the adjoining sanctuary of San Giorgio. In the apse glass-fronted cupboards display skulls attached to child-sized dolls. These are, or were, bits of Christian martyrs, and their infantilization seems a tough reward for those who died for their beliefs. Opposite the sanctuary, steps lead to a terrace offering more fine views over the sadly urbanized plain, and at the summit of the hill is the Rocca, the ruined fortress of Monselice.

A few kilometres west of Monselice lies the bustling little town of Este. Yet within the walls of the *castello* all is tranquil – except when the fairground is in operation – for this is now the city park, which was laid out in 1848 by the versatile architect Japelli, who made such an impact on Padua. Behind the *castello* are a number of fine and well-concealed villas, including the Villa de Kunkler where Byron lived from 1817 to 1818, and where Shelley, while Byron's guest, wrote his 'Lines Written Among the Euganean Hills'. Este is among the most ancient Veneto towns, and enjoyed a thriving Stone Age culture well before the Romans took control.

For two centuries Este was one of the most powerful cities in northern Italy, dominating not only many other cities of the Veneto but large areas of what is now Emilia-Romagna to the south. After the decline of the house of Este, the usual crowd of medieval warlords, including the Scaligeri, the Visconti, and the Carraresi, ran the city until it became part of the Venetian empire in 1405. There has been a castle here since the eleventh century, but the surviving towers and wall are mostly the work of the Carraresi under Umberto da Carrara in the 1340s. Just inside the walls is an archaeological museum of considerable interest. The upstairs rooms document the indigenous local culture of the region, mostly thanks to excavations from necropolises dating from 900–400 BC: the exhibits include bronze vases and implements, ceramics and jewellery, and figurines intended as votive offerings. Downstairs the museum

The sanctuary of San Giorgio beneath the fortress at Monselice.

chronicles the gradual submersion of the Este culture by the increasingly dominant Roman civilization. Among the prize exhibits are a small but vivid bronze of the head of Medusa and elegant mosaic floors. The final room contains medieval exhibits, including part of a fine fresco of the Crucifixion and a powerful polychrome *Pietà*.

On leaving the museum, turn right until you reach the cathedral, an ungainly brick oval structure built in 1701 on the site of earlier churches. The interior is far

A southerly hill of the Colli Euganei at Calaone near Este.

Right **The theatre at Lendinara.**

more successful. In the choir hangs a large painting by G. B. Tiepolo depicting Santa Tecla successfully persuading God to liberate Este from the plague in 1630. In a south chapel a finely carved fifteenth-century pulpit is attached to the wall, and the church also possesses an eloquent Crucifix.

A magnificent renaissance arch just outside Este.

From the church Via Cavour leads back into the centre. As you cross Piazza Maggiore you will see on the right the bulky shape of the seventeenth-century clock-tower. Continue straight on to the churches of San Martino, with its dangerously leaning campanile, and Santa Maria delle Grazie, which was rebuilt in the eighteenth century. The latter's only interesting feature is a byzantine-style image of the Virgin and Child in the choir that reputedly performs miracles.

From Este head south-west to the hamlet of Carceri and its abbey, founded in the eleventh century by Azzo II of Este. The precincts are entered through a fortified gateway. The abbey church was rebuilt in the seventeenth century in an austere neo-classical style, and of the medieval church, only two sides of a romanesque cloister remain, separating the church from the elegant and lofty drive-in cloister built in the sixteenth century.

From Carceri drive south to Lendinara. Just outside the town centre is the mostly seventeenth-century

sanctuary of Madonna del Pilastrello. In the north aisle is a painting of the *Ascension with Donor* (1581) by the School of Veronese. The *duomo*, Santa Sofia, is a big dark eighteenth-century church, and I have never managed to gain access to the sacristy, where the best paintings are kept. The town has a moderately picturesque main piazza. On one corner are the remains of the Este castle, and opposite it the modest town hall with its loggia below.

Continue south to Fratta Polesine. On either side of its church are two obelisked villas, but continue to the edge of town and you'll soon see Palladio's Villa Badoer (1556), commissioned, like so many of these country seats, by a Venetian grandee. Its broad pedimented portico of six Ionic columns is approached by three shallow sets of steps, from which other steps lead to the colonnaded barchesse wings. The portico and interior have badly damaged frescoes that are decorative enough but hardly of exceptional quality. The villa is empty and poorly maintained, and in such condition a sixteenth-century villa, even one by Palladio, can seem bleak: a symmetrical collection of tall rooms, and no plumbing in sight. Later that century was built Villa Bragadin, which stands at right angles to Badoer, and is a more modest version of La Malcontenta.

A few kilometres further south is Fiesso Umbertiano. Its airy church has a fine coffered ceiling of 1691, each panel painted with angels or religious scenes. Not far from here is the octagon-topped eighteenth-century Palazzo Vendramin by Andrea Tirali. On the road out of town to the east is a bizarre villa with two curved gables, which looks seventeenth-century.

Just south of Fiesso join the *autostrada* and drive north to the Terme Euganee exit, than drive west to Valnogaredo. Here the church has a sprightly façade of 1758 with statues by Antonio Bonazza, and opposite it stands the spacious Villa Piva, its walls also adorned with statues. From here there's a tricky drive west to Valbona, the site of a fortress-like castle, constructed

The thirteenth-century castle at Valbona is exceptionally well preserved.

Left The façade of the monastery church at Praglia, a major Benedictine foundation.

Above A statue of the Madonna at Praglia, the immense Benedictine monastery near Padua.

in the thirteenth century and the property of the Carraresi from 1340 onwards, and subsequently of a succession of great Venetian families. It exhibits a pleasing fusion of elements: towers, battlements, galleries, and, of course, massive stone and brick walls.

From Valbona head north to Vo Vecchio, with its pleasantly arcaded square. On the other side of the road is the ugly Villa Contarini Venier, and at nearby Zovon Villa Mariani dominates the hillside. The road continues north-east towards Padua, passing the monastery of Praglia, set against one of the hump-like hills of the Colli Euganei. This great Benedictine foundation of the early twelfth century, although no buildings from that period survive, was secularized by Napoleon, but returned to the Benedictines in 1834; expelled again in 1867, they came back again in 1904. Except for the campanile, all buildings date from 1460 or later. A broad flight of steps leads to the piazza in front of the church, which was completed in 1548 and has an elaborate façade that is essentially the creation of Tullio Lombardo. The interior is dignified and austere, and surprisingly delicate, thanks to the notably thin square piers with Ionic capitals. Apart from a wooden crucifix in a north aisle chapel, most of the works of art are preserved in the choir. The sixteenth-century choir stalls are richly carved, and suspended from the frescoed dome is an exquisite fourteenth-century cross, painted on both sides, from the school of Giotto.

The monastery may be visited in the company of one of the monks, who will show you not only the church but the splendid fifteenth-century cloister, the *botanico*, which is overlooked by stylish Venetian-gothic windows. Herbs were grown in the *botanico*, and the monastery still produces and markets a large range of herbal concoctions. From the cloister a lovely renaissance portal leads to a staircase, built in 1712, which in turn leads up to another cloister, the more

austere Chiostro Pensile. A marble well of 1559 stands in the centre. From this cloister there is an excellent view of the campanile, built in about 1350 but much restored and rebuilt. The Chiostro Pensile is the heart of the monastery, as from here there is access to the dormitory, the church, the chapterhouse, the kitchens and refectory, and the library and scriptorium. Praglia, now inhabited by fifty monks, is known for its skills in the restoration of ancient books and manuscripts. The magnificent refectory, furnished in 1726 by Bartolomeo Biasi, is lined with beautifully carved walnut and briar stalls. The structure on one side of the door is the mirror image of that on the other, a kind of negative/positive effect. Outside the refectory are ravishing washbasins designed by Tullio Lombardo, and consisting of inlays of lead and marble. The very fine painting of the *Crucifixion* at the head of the hall (monks are seated in order of their initiation into monastic life) is the work of Bartolommeo Montagna (*c*.1450–1523). Zelotti, the Veronese artist who frescoed the dome of the church, contributed paintings along the refectory walls. The pulpit half-way along is by Tullio Lombardo.

The cloister also leads to a loggia, which overlooks the abbey's vineyards and beehives and allows a discreet view of the monks' cells: fully paid-up monks on the upper floors, novices below. Sadly, the two other cloisters are not accessible to the public, and neither is the splendid eighteenth-century library. Nonetheless a visit to Praglia is most rewarding, for few of the monasteries of the Veneto are open to the public. Indeed, many monks give the impression of deriving particular pleasure from rewarding the tourist who has driven at a snail's pace up a winding single-track road with a stern notice denying access. At Praglia, however, I found a warm welcome, even though I turned up minutes before visiting hours ended. I was given a long and leisurely tour by a studious Benedictine father, who expressed no resentment at putting time at my disposal.

Praglia is only a short drive from Padua, despite its rural surroundings in the hills, and, logically, it is only a short drive back to the city.

The art of country living: the exquisite Villa delle Rose near Tramonte.

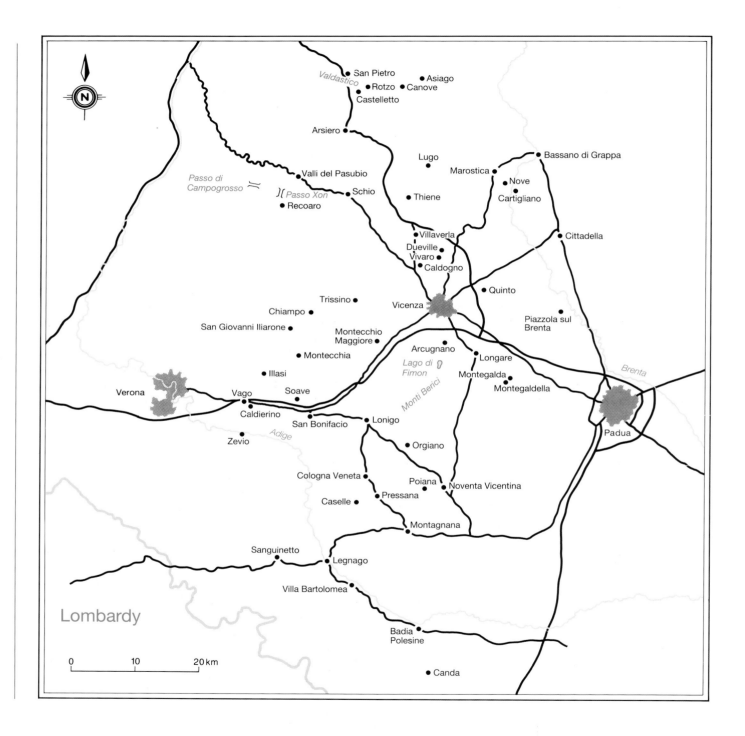

San Pietro
Valdastico
Rotzo
Castelletto
Asiago
Canove
Arsiero
Lugo
Bassano di Grappa
Valli del Pasubio
Marostica
Nove
Passo di Campogrosso
Passo Xon
Schio
Cartigliano
Recoaro
Thiene
Villaverla
Cittadella
Dueville
Vivaro
Caldogno
Trissino
Quinto
Chiampo
Vicenza
San Giovanni Iliarone
Piazzola sul Brenta
Montecchio Maggiore
Arcugnano
Montecchia
Longare
Lago di Fimon
Illasi
Montegalda
Verona
Soave
Montegaldella
Vago
Brenta
Caldierino
San Bonifacio
Lonigo
Monti Berici
Padua
Zevio
Adige
Orgiano
Cologna Veneta
Poiana
Noventa Vicentina
Caselle
Pressana
Montagnana
Sanguinetto
Legnago
Villa Bartolomea
Lombardy
Badia Polesine
Canda

0   10   20 km

4
Vicenza and the Central Veneto
Vicenza—Montagnana—Soave—Thiene—the Valdastico—Marostica

Vicenza is invariably thought of as the city of Palladio (1508–80), and with good reason. But there is more to this very pleasant city, for although it is less grandiose and less obviously an urban powerhouse than either Padua or Verona, it has a very marked character of its own. Originally a Gaulish settlement along the banks of the rivers Retrone and Bacchiglione, it became the Roman town of Vicetia, and the street plan was laid out at this time. Medieval Vicenza, like Padua, participated in the battles against Holy Roman Emperor Frederick Barbarossa. Unfortunately, the city did not come well out of the struggle, and was largely destroyed in 1236. For most of the fourteenth century it was under the control of the Scaligeri, and after a brief period of Visconti rule, it sought the protection of Venice in 1404. The city's troubles were not over, and Vicenza was involved in often bloody power struggles, usually as a result of being in the wrong place at the wrong time. Vicenza remained under Venetian control until 1813, when the Austrians occupied the city; finally, in 1866, Vicenza became part of the reunified nation of Italy.

Because of the almost constant state of war, not to mention bouts of plague, that preoccupied Vicenza until the 1530s, the city was late in undertaking the kind of renaissance civic building programmes that contributed to the urban pride of its larger neighbours.

The young Palladio was thus unwittingly provided with precisely the kinds of opportunities an aspiring architect needed at the outset of his career, and these allowed him to stamp his artistic personality so firmly on this little city of, at that time, no more than 20,000 inhabitants. By birth and training, Palladio, whose real name was Andrea di Pietro, was Paduan. He was given his famous sobriquet by his patron Count Trissino, who also took him to Rome, a formative influence in the artistic development of the young. north Italian. Palladio made his reputation in the 1540s as a designer of villas in the countryside around Vicenza. But it was two urban commissions in Vicenza itself that were to establish him once and for all as a major architect: the Palazzo Thiene, and the so-called Basilica.

Since there is considerable variety within his *œuvre* it is not easy to define those elements of his work that are distinctly and unmistakably 'Palladian'. Perhaps the unifying factor in all his work is a sense of interrelationship, sometimes in the most methodical geometrical sense, between the different elements in his architectural vocabulary. This is an expression of an acute sense of order; there is nothing superfluous, nothing frivolously fanciful, in a building by Palladio. Everything is purposeful, dignified, ordered, connected. This can lead to a certain austerity, and many of the ornaments now decorating some of his buildings

are later additions by other hands and not part of the original design. Another, less tangible, unifying factor is a sense of power that I discern in his finest buildings. The tight interrelationship between the various architectural elements confers a tremendous sense of pent-up force. His designs are both harmonious and, in an almost mystical sense, imploded. What is extraordinary is that despite a deliberately restricted neo-classical architectural vocabulary, he hardly ever repeated a design. Above all else, Palladio is an architect of constantly astonishing originality.

Cars are banned from the city centre of Vicenza, but it is usually easy to park near the railway station, from where it is a short walk to the Porta Castello, the principal gateway to the city from the direction of Verona. On the left you will see an immense brick machicolated tower of the eleventh century, all that remains of a Scaliger fortress. The Porta Castello leads directly to Corso Palladio, the main street of the old town. On the right, about a block away, is the *duomo*. As in Padua, the cathedral is far from being the most interesting church of the city. Vicenza's *duomo* suffered from extensive damage during World War II. The stepped façade of 1467 with its diapered marble pattern and its rosette window survived the bombing, but most of the church did not, and much of the building has been reconstructed. The interior is an aisleless hall with plain gothic rib vaulting and numerous side chapels. The choir, on a raised platform over the crypt, is lit by six lancets filled with poor-quality stained glass.

Among the side chapels of the south aisle, the first has an eighth-century trough-like sarcophagus. The fifth houses a much darkened polyptych of 1356 by Lorenzo Veneziano. Among the north chapels, the fourth contains a bored-looking *Madonna* by Bartolommeo Montagna, Vicenza's best-known painter, and the fifth houses pompous sixteenth-century tombs and a stylized polychrome relief of the coronation of the

The exquisite Casa Pigafetta at Vicenza belonged to one of Magellan's fellow explorers.

A detail from the Casa Pigafetta, where late gothic design meets the Renaissance.

Virgin by the fifteenth-century artist Antonino da Venezia. Adjoining the crypt are subterranean rooms that date back to the eighth century, but they appear to be permanently closed.

Emerging from the south door you can see the detached eleventh-century campanile on the left, and to the right of Piazza del Duomo stands the Loggia Zeno. Across the piazza is the entrance to the Roman Criptoporticus, a subterranean portico of a former villa which is hardly ever open to visitors. Walk past the campanile into the small piazza and the arcaded Contrà Peschiere Vecchia. (Contrà is a Venetian word for Via, and is used throughout Vicenza.) At the end, turn right, then left into Contrà Pigafetta. The lovely Casa Pigafetta is an early renaissance mansion (1481), named after one of Magellan's companions on his globe-encircling voyage. Despite a proliferation of gothic trefoils, the spirit of this pink marble gem is clearly renaissance, with delightful low-relief medallions

137

between the windows and trilobed balconies supported on griffins and cornucopias; it is an exceedingly pretty mansion. At the end of the lane, turn left into Piazza delle Erbe, and you will now be facing one side of Palladio's Basilica, which was commissioned in 1549 but not completed until 1617, many years after his death. Connected to the Basilica by a lofty bridge of 1493, the Arco degli Zavattieri, is the early medieval Torre del Girone, the tall prison tower, still with heavy iron bars on its windows. Mount the steps and walk through the building into the Piazza dei Signori, the large central square that was once the site of the Roman forum.

You will now be standing alongside the Basilica. The term suggests an ecclesiastical building, but Palladio was referring to ancient buildings where justice was meted out. This hall, the meeting place of the city's Council of the Five Hundred, is of gothic origin, but Palladio surrounded it with loggias on two ample storeys, and encased the roof in diapered marble, pink and white. Like the Palazzo della Ragione in Padua, Vicenza's Basilica had been surrounded with loggias in the 1420s, but the original loggias collapsed later that century and it was the need to replace them that formed the core of Palladio's commission. Palladio was not the obvious choice as architect. For years the Council had engaged in discussions with some of northern Italy's leading architects, and it may well be a combination of local reputation and the influence of his patrons that secured Palladio this vitally important commission.

The top of Palladio's structure is balustraded and each of the columns that divide the nine bays is topped with a statue. Palladio varied the design of each storey: the lower has round arches resting on plain Doric capitals but with a lightly ornamented frieze above, while the upper level has Ionic volutes but no frieze. This grand composition has its ardent admirers, and there is something compelling about the almost sym-

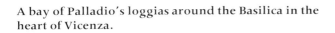

A bay of Palladio's loggias around the Basilica in the heart of Vicenza.

Steps lead up to a Palladian masterpiece, the Basilica at Vicenza.

bolic fashion in which Palladio clothed a gothic shell in these newly woven renaissance garments. But in the flesh, as it were, it does lack a certain warmth, like so much of Palladio's work. A flight of steps ascends to the first floor and the immense hall within. It has a fine wooden roof, and its ribs, resembling carved rope, rest on ornamental corbels.

Next to the Basilica is a huge slender clock-tower, embellished with the winged lion of St Mark, an emblem repeated on one of the two columns at the end of the piazza. This tower is of early medieval origin but the upper stages were added in 1331 and 1444. Behind it is a small piazza and on the right the Gothic Domus Comestabilis, where the Venetian *podestà* lived. Opposite the tower is the façade of the church of San Vincenzo, whose two-storeyed loggia echoes the theme of the Basilica; but the ornamentation is far more vociferous, with Corinthian capitals and with angels and languishing women in each spandrel of the six arches. On either side of the church are the wings of the arcaded Monte di Pietà. The building next to it with four immense brick Corinthian half-columns rising the height of its two main storeys is Palladio's Loggia del Capitaniato; the façade facing the Monte di Pietà is lavishly decorated with reliefs and statues that celebrate the great Venetian victory over the Turks at Lepanto. This loggia is the most flashy of Palladio's town houses, with its soaring columns, jutting balconies, and big-toothed cornices; here is just a hint of classicism peering round the corner towards the baroque.

Beyond the two pillars at the end of the square is Piazza delle Biade and the church of the Servi, a leading centre of Mariolatry. Despite its renaissance façade of 1531, it dates from the century before. It has a handsome interior with pointed arches and rib vaults constructed from broad bands of stone and brick. Along the aisle wall is a good collection of renaissance altars. The door to the sacristy also leads to the renaissance cloister, a pleasant if unremarkable ensemble with a varied set of capitals. It is now used as a repository for weathered church statues and as a parking area.

Return to Corso Palladio by bearing right after you leave the church. To the left on the Corso is the narrow but very tall white stone façade of San Gaetano (1728), much damaged in World War II and since rebuilt. Continue down the Corso. On the left you will soon come to the Dominican church of Santa Corona, built in the 1260s, although the choir dates from the Renaissance. (There are fine *palazzi* along Contrà Santa Corona, and further up the lane in which the church stands is the much altered Palazzo Leoni-Montanara by Longhena.) Constructed of brick, Santa Corona has a particularly elaborate and stylish campanile. The fenestration and brickwork have been thoroughly renewed, as has the aisled interior, but the main appeal of the church lies in its superb contents.

Along the south aisle, the fourth chapel contains an elaborate *Adoration of the Magi* (1573) by Veronese. The fifth chapel is filled with over thirty seventeenth-century panels mostly by the School of Maganza, the paintings fanning out along the ceiling; the principal canvases celebrate Venetian triumphs. Against the east wall of the aisle is a noble medieval Crucifix, and next to it in the Cappella Thiene are two hefty late gothic wall-tombs with slanted effigies in armour. Corberelli's high altar (1669), flanked by statues, is a complex marvel of inlaid coloured marbles. Panels depict the Resurrection and the Last Supper as well as secular still lifes and cornucopias. From close up you can see that much of the draughtsmanship is feeble, but from afar the altar does indeed look splendid. Curiously, it is just as elaborate on the reverse side. The lovely choir stalls, with inlaid veneer panels of architectural scenes as well as still lifes, date from the 1480s. Part of the crypt consists of an austere side chapel, Cappella Valmarana, designed by Palladio. Note how the corner pilasters have been bent so that they divide at right angles in order to squeeze into the space available.

In the north aisle, the second chapel has a fine *Mary Magdalen and Saints* by Bartolommeo Montagna, the most renowned native artist. In the south chapel, an anonymous painting of about 1500 incorporates a view of Vicenza. The fifth chapel contains one of the most beautiful Venetian paintings outside Venice: Giovanni Bellini's *Baptism of Christ*, set against a background of hills and castles. In stark contrast is the painting in the north transept, *Christ Crowned with Thorns*, by Tentorello, its coarse faces and primitive energy worlds away from the elegance and serenity of Bellini, but not to be despised on that account. (I have attempted, in numerous libraries, to find out more about this fourteenth-century painter, but without any success; he appears not even to have been consigned a footnote in art history.) The church's famous medieval reliquary containing one of the thorns from Christ's Crown of Thorns is displayed only on special occasions, such as Good Friday.

At the end of Corso Palladio is the brick building – a

Facing the Basilica of Vicenza is another of Palladio's buildings, the Loggia del Capitaniato.

kind of domesticated fortress – known as the Territorio. Walk through its pleasant forecourt to reach the Teatro Olimpico, Palladio's astonishing last work (1580), the construction of which was supervised by his pupil and rival Vincenzo Scamozzi. (The Tempietto at Maser was also completed after Palladio's death; see p. 90.) The theatre was commissioned by the Accademia Olimpia, a learned society founded in 1555 by Palladio himself and twenty local scholars and aristocrats, with the aim of furthering the cultivation of the arts and sciences. There are two halls to cross before one reaches the auditorium. One is the Odeon, with its now somewhat pallid frescoes honouring the Academy; the other is the ante-Odeon, with interesting sixteenth-century monochrome frescoes celebrating famous performances at the theatre.

These ante-rooms can't prepare one for the splendour of the auditorium itself. Its semicircular tiers are backed by a colonnade of stucco and wood, filled with two tiers of statues. Yet even this is nothing compared to the structure that fills the breadth and height of the stage itself: a classical extravaganza of Corinthian columns and pediments, crammed with statues, some in rectangular niches, others free-standing. Some of the statuary alludes to the Labours of Hercules; some portrays Palladio's contemporaries. Also made from stucco and wood, this immense yet deft edifice, reminiscent of Roman triumphal arches, masquerades as solid stone. Two rectangular entrances flank the central arched opening, and through each we see, from wherever we are sitting in the auditorium, Scamozzi's three-dimensional sets, painted and rendered in perspective to persuade us that we have before us a renaissance recreation of ancient Thebes, executed for the opening performance at the theatre in 1585 of Sophocles' *Oedipus Tyrannus*. The richly coffered ceiling over the stage, painted only in 1914, is rendered in muted tones that do not distract from the splendours below. Surely the Teatro Olimpico is the world's most theatrical theatre?

To this rhetorical question, the American novelist, James Fennimore Cooper, whom we have already encountered making crass observations about the Brenta canal, would give a negative response. In his view, 'who but a bungler would put eyes in a statue, give a real perspective to a picture ... or real streets to a theatre? ... The thing, as a matter of course, was a failure.'

Across the piazza from the theatre is the Palazzo Chiericati of 1550, one of Palladio's more cheerful and complete designs, with its corner loggias and arcades and statues. Since 1855 it has housed the Museo Civico, with its rich collections of paintings and archaeological remains. Bartolommeo Montagna is well represented, and among other Veneto artists included are Cima da Conegliano, Veronese, Tintoretto, and the Bassano family. More surprising inclusions are paintings by Flemish painters Hans Memling (1430/40–94) and Bruegel the Elder.

To explore Vicenza's townscape in more detail, return to the other end of the Corso and continue beyond Porta Castello for a few hundred yards, until you reach the basilica – an ecclesiastical one, the genuine article – of Santi Felice e Fortunato. Enter the forecourt, with its scattered sarcophagi, and you will see the remarkable twelfth-century fortified campanile, with its octagonal top. The façade of the stately church is probably even earlier, from the tenth century. Over the portal are fairly vivid remains of thirteenth-century frescoes. The aisled interior is broad and dignified, and half-way down the nave are remains of the mosaic floor from the fifth-century basilica that used to stand here. I had hoped, after a service, to visit the crypt and the fourth-century martyrium. The priest insisted on closing up immediately and said if I wanted to see anything of interest I could find it outside the church as much as within it. I found this smug old man so rude that I have had to boycott his church and have never returned.

Walk back towards the city centre along Borgo San Felice and before Porta Castello you will pass the late sixteenth-century park, the Giardino Salvi. In the west

Dazzling sets fill the stage at Palladio's justly celebrated Teatro Olimpico in Vicenza.

corner is the contemporary Palladian Loggia Valmarana, perched over a canal, and at the other end of the waterway in the park is Longhena's even simpler loggia of 1649. Just after Porta Castello, you will see on the right, at the end of the plaza, the two extant bays, tall and disproportionate because incomplete, of Palazzo Porto-Breganza, probably designed by Palladio and continued by Scamozzi. Corso Palladio is lined with splendid mansions, and no. 13, Palazzo Bonin, is attributed to Scamozzi. At no. 47 is the much restored gothic Palazzo Thiene. Turn left into Contrà Fogazzaro. No. 16 is Palladio's superb Palazzo Valmarana-Braga. Note how the giant pilasters appear to rip apart the lower pilasters, how the cornice juts over each capital, how the statues at either end frame the building despite the less emphatic modelling of the outer bays.

Continue up the street, keeping an eye out for *pasticcerie* that sell *fugazza vicentina*, the Easter cake that is the city's contribution to the vast repertoire of biscuits and cakes of the Veneto. Soon you will reach the church of San Lorenzo, which was secularized in 1797 and returned to the Franciscan order only in 1927. On either side of its superb façade, canopied tombs flank a magnificent gothic portal, lintel, and tympanum, all richly carved and couched beneath soaring blind arcades. The mighty interior has arcades resting on stout round pillars; stone arches span the choir chapels. The only jarring note is the clumsy rib-vaulting of the aisles. The choir and its side chapels are filled with mostly renaissance tombs. In the south transept is a striking late fifteenth-century polychrome altar-piece, carved rather than painted; and there are more finely carved altar statues in the north choir. Most of the frescoes are in very poor condition. The north transept leads to a charming fifteenth-century cloister, where the delicate double windows of the chapter house add an elegant touch. On leaving the church by the west door, spare a glance for the bombastic militaristic baroque tomb of 1661 over the door.

The sumptuous Gothic tympanum at the church of San Lorenzo in Vicenza.

The building opposite the church is Francesco Muttoni's Palazzo Repeta of 1710. As you continue up Contrà Fogazzaro, note how many of the street arcades rest on earlier capitals. You soon reach Santa Maria del Carmine; its interior is lined with a wonderfully complete set of renaissance carved altar niches from an earlier church. The first chapel in the north aisle, especially fine, contains an altar-piece of about 1530 by Benedetto Montagna (1481–1558), son of Bartolomeo. Returning to Corso Palladio, you'll see at no. 67 the Venetian-gothic Palazzo Brunello. The attribution of Palazzo Poiana at no. 94 to Palladio is unsubstantiated. The splendid Palazzo Trissino-Baston at no. 98, with its lofty Ionic arcade and elegant upper storeys and airy courtyard, was begun by Scamozzi in about 1592. Turn left into Contrada Porti. At no. 8 is the elaborate Venetian-gothic Palazzo Cavelloni-Thiene. No. 11, Palazzo Porto-Barbarana, was designed by Palladio and enlivened with reliefs and medallions in a style more rich than Palladio usually sanctioned.

Contrada Porti must be as richly stuffed with *palazzi* as any lane in Italy. Quite apart from the Palazzo Porto-Barbarana, you'll find at no. 12 a *palazzo* with a fine renaissance portal, at no. 14 the Venetian-gothic Palazzo Trissino-Sperotti, and at no. 17 the even grander late-gothic Palazzo Porto-Breganze, with its fine loggia over the courtyard. No. 19, the Palazzo Colleoni-Porto, is also Venetian-gothic in style, as is no. 27. Next to the Palazzo Colleoni-Porto, at no. 21, is the austere Palazzo Iseppo da Porto of 1552, attributed to Palladio. Originally the interior was frescoed by Veronese and Zelotti; these decorations have long vanished, though a much restored ceiling by G. B. Tiepolo survives. By now it will be apparent that Vicenza is very much a city of façades, of ambitions that could not always be sustained. Many of these palaces, including some designed by Palladio, were never completed. Even the famous Basilica is not a complete composition, but a dazzling cloak thrown over the shoulders of an existing building.

Return to the Corso, and turn left up Contrà San Gaetano, which becomes Contrà Zanella. On the left as you turn the corner you see the rear façade of Palazzo

Thiene, a deeply rusticated and severe composition by Palladio. A sixteenth-century architectural equivalent of power dressing, this is power building, based on Roman rather than north Italian models, and the same is true of the courtyard. On the right you will find the church of San Stefano; in the north transept hangs an altar-piece of the 1520s by Palma Vecchio, in rich Venetian colours, one of the artist's major works. His real name was Jacopo Negreti, and he was born in Bergamo in about 1480. His style is thoroughly Venetian, even Titianesque. His best works, such as this altar-piece, glow with colour, though they can be curiously placid and inexpressive, lacking the high drama of, say, Veronese. Opposite San Stefano is the rather battered late fifteenth-century Palazzo Negri, and next to it the more delicate Venetian-gothic Casa Fontana. Return to the Corso.

At no. 147 you come to the large *palazzo* known as the Ca' d'Oro. The entrance passage contains a small lapidary collection assembled in the nineteenth century. Continue down the Corso to Piazza Matteoti, where the Teatro Olimpico is located, and bear right past the Museo Civico into Contrà Cabianco. This leads past more gothic and renaissance *palazzi* (no. 6 is especially charming). Turn left down Contrà Ponte San Michele, lingering on the bridge over the River Retrone to enjoy the views. On the left is the oratory of San Nicolò, which is stuffed with eighteenth-century paintings but rarely open. Continue for a short distance, then turn right, and return via another bridge, passing at no. 17 Contrà Pescaria a frescoed gothic *palazzo*, to the Piazza delle Erbe.

Easily visible from Vicenza is the hilltop campanile of the Sanctuary of Monte Berico, which sprang into existence after visions of the Virgin Mary in the 1420s. It makes a satisfying starting point for this first itinerary out of Vicenza, a drive that will explore the region south of the city. The sanctuary church, although late gothic at its core, mostly consists of a

Greek-cross-shaped church by Carlo Borella (1688). The image of the crowned Madonna over the high altar dates from the fifteenth century. The sanctuary, while not immune from the piety-laden atmosphere to which pilgrimage sites are vulnerable, does contain some very fine works of art. To the right is a superb *Pietà* by Bartolommeo Montagna, whose smaller fresco on the same theme transfigures the sacristy. A north chapel contains fine, if inaccessible, late fifteenth-century inlaid choir stalls. The Sala di Quadro near the sacristy has two incongruous tenants: a fossil collection and, more importantly, a lush masterpiece by Veronese, the *Banquet of St Gregory* (1572). Austrian soldiers turned the great canvas into rags in 1848, but the painting was restored on the orders of none other than Emperor Franz Josef of Austria (1848–1916).

From the sanctuary, descend the road alongside the eighteenth-century *portici* that climb the hill. These 150 arcades are the work of Francesco Muttoni. Then bear right, and, on foot, take the lane alongside the high wall that leads to Villa Valmarana ai Nani. After about 300 m you will see the dwarfish statues on the wall alongside the villa, a plain building of 1668 by Antonio Muttoni set within a small park. There is a touching and thoroughly improbable legend that the estate belonged to a nobleman whose daughter was a dwarf. To encourage her in the false belief that she was of normal height, he had her brought up solely by other dwarves. Inevitably, the girl eventually laid eyes on a handsome horseman of the correct proportions and, realizing the well-meant trick that had been played on her, put an end to her life.

Many of the rooms, in the guest house as well as the villa itself, are enriched with frescoes of classical and mythological scenes by both Tiepolos, with Giambattista responsible for much of the decoration in the villa and Giovanni Domenico for the adornment of the guest house. The freshness of Giovanni Domenico's work is outstanding, and is seen to best advantage in the *chinoiserie* room of the guest house. He is often overshadowed by his prolific father, but not at Valmarana.

A path opposite the entrance to the villa leads to La

A detail from one of the dozens of beautiful *palazzi* at Vicenza.

Rotonda, Palladio's great and immensely influential hilltop villa of 1566. Its size is as surprising as its simplicity of design, with its four identical façades, each with a pedimented portico reached up a flight of steps. The shallow cupola reflects the fact that the central hall is indeed a rotunda, lavishly decorated with frescoes. Most of Palladio's villas are related to, or even attached to, agricultural buildings, making them rural residences with a direct connection to the local economy. This is not the case at La Rotonda, which was evidently designed solely as a pleasure dome. It has been a major tourist attraction more or less from the time of its completion, and other architects adopted it as a model. Not only are the English country houses of Chiswick House and Mereworth Castle based on La Rotonda, but comparable structures in the United States and Russia are more loosely modelled on it.

The best view of the cubical exterior is from the road called the Riviera Berici (SS247) which traverses the valley beneath it, heading south. You can make a detour to the right to Arcugnano, driving through the lovely gentle Berici hills, which are of volcanic origin; along the Vicenza road here is the Villa Pasini, built in 1770 by Ottavio Scamozzi (1719–90). Its loggia extends to the attic storey, and the gardens are delightful. You can wander at leisure through the hills – Lago di Fimon is a good spot to head for – or return to the Riviera Berici and head south to Longare.

Take the right turn for Costozza. On the right you will see Villa Trento Carli, with its handsome, somewhat overblown façade. Around the corner on the right are the Ville di Schio, three villas set within flamboyant terraced gardens; and opposite is Villa Eolia, now doubling as a Zelotti-frescoed restaurant.

Return to the SS247 and cross it in the direction of Montegalda. This village is overlooked by the creamy asymmetrical mass of the castle, which dates from 1176. In the eighteenth century it was converted into an elaborate villa and surrounded with fine gardens.

For centuries pilgrims have been climbing the hill from Vicenza to the Sanctuary at Monte Berico.

Statues of dwarves line the walls of the Villa Valmarana ai Nani near Vicenza.

Just south of here is Montegaldella, where you'll find the early seventeenth-century Villa Conti-Campagnolo, known as La Deliziosa. It's a dramatic and grand villa, with a very tall portico. An immense cloister arcade frames the gardens, which are lavishly embellished with statues by Orazio Marinali (1643–1720); his work is also abundantly represented at the Ville di Schio in Costozza and at the Sanctuary of Monte Berico.

Return to the SS247 and head south. Shortly before Noventa Vicentina, turn left on Via Finale. You will soon come to the unfinished and gaunt Villa Saraceno Lombardi, attributed to Palladio. A few hundred metres along the same road is Sammicheli's Villa Saraceno Bettanin of 1550, now part of a farmstead. In the centre of Noventa itself is the Villa Barbarigo, now the town hall, a coarse colonnaded structure of about 1600. Just west of Noventa on the southern edge of Poiana is Palladio's idiosyncratic Villa Poiana of 1555.

Above **Palladio's best-known villa, La Rotonda, dominates a hilltop near Vicenza.**

Right **In spring many Veneto vineyards are carpeted with flowers that will later be ploughed in to the soil.**

The rounded arch with a band of *oculi* (eye-shaped windows) around the portal is a most curious device, at odds with the formality of the pediment topped with statues. The interior is frescoed. Opposite the villa stands another older villa with a fourteenth-century tower. From Poiana it's a short drive south to Montagnana.

Montagnana is entirely surrounded by two kilometres of medieval walls and 24 towers, begun by Ezzelino in the thirteenth century and completed on the orders of Francesco I da Carrara. Their main purpose was to keep the Scaligeri at bay. During Venice's war against the League of Cambrai in 1509, Montagnana was unable to cope, and the city changed hands thirteen times. Nowadays the little town devotes itself, among other activities, to the production of excellent *prosciutto crudo*.

Four gateways lead into the town. The walls are not only well preserved but sheltered from traffic, as they once were from hostile forces, by a wide grassy fosse. A broad passageway runs between the inside of the walls and the houses, except for one patch where the houses are built right up against the fortifications. Just before entering the town through the complex Padua gate, you'll see on the right, hemmed in by roads and other buildings, the Villa Pisani (1565), designed by Palladio. This boxy and rather dilapidated mansion is easy to identify since the name of Federico Pisani is engraved in huge letters beneath the pediment. The rear view from the garden is more attractive, showing the portico below with Doric capitals, the loggia above with Ionic. The façade overlooking the road has the same orders, but no open spaces.

The main square in the town centre is loosely surrounded by a number of houses with gothic arcades. The west front of the *duomo* is a great unadorned mass of brick, broken only by a fine clock and by a renaissance portal attributed both to Sansovino and to Sammicheli. The interior is equally gaunt

In Montagnana, houses have been built alongside the medieval walls that encircle the town.

despite the paintings and the unusual feature of rounded transepts. The altar-piece, a *Transfiguration*, is by Veronese. Veneto towns are filled with depictions of the great naval victory at Lepanto over the Turks, and one of the most painstaking is here on the north wall. On the south wall are two large canvases by Giovanni Buonconsiglio (*c*.1470–*c*.1535), and above the choir stalls skilful seventeenth-century paintings by Massimo da Verona.

Turn left on leaving the *duomo*, then left again at the piazza corner and you will soon see on your right the rectangular block of the town hall, with its tall arcades and severe neo-classical doorways. This too is partly the work of Sammicheli. One wet afternoon I encountered in a room beneath the town hall children brandishing swords and other accessories, making early preparations for the local Palio; stuffed into the room was a sufficient number of helmets, pikes, drums, crossbows, and banners to equip a major battle. Not far away, on the southern edge of the old town, is the fourteenth-century church of San Francesco with its fine campanile. Just before leaving Montagnana by the western gate, you'll see on the right a charming Lombard-style *palazzo* with pretty balconies and elegantly fluted pilasters around the windows. The western gate, the Rocca degli Alberi, is even more splendid than the Padua gate. It was built by the Carraresi and boasts a fine tower.

Drive south to Badia Polesine. Park in the large Piazza Marconi and walk into the pedestrian street near the Pasticceria Sanremo. You will soon reach the town hall and church in Piazza Vittorio Emanuele. Continue into Via San Alberto until you reach the splendid and partly fortified Venetian-gothic Palazzo degli Estensi. Beyond it you will glimpse the Abbazia della Vangadizza, Badia's most important monument, on the right. Near the sealed rear entrance you will find, partly concealed by shrubbery, the eleventh-century sarcophagi of members of the Este family. The abbey itself is dominated by a tall brick campanile topped by a conical tower. A passage leads from the shabby forecourt into the cloister, on the far side of which is a door (usually marked closed but try it

Left The stylish renaissance portal of the cathedral at Montagnana.

Above A Venetian-gothic well-head graces the cloister of Abbazia della Vangadizza at Badia Polesine.

Wooden doors, iron balconies, stone walls: a Veneto townscape at Legnago.

anyway) leading into a garden from which one can approach both the campanile and the large half-ruined fifteenth-century chapel of the Virgin Mary, topped by a stout brick drum. The refectory is now used as an art gallery. The irregular cloister, with its upper loggia, is the most attractive feature of the abbey. The slender columns supporting the loggia roof are of marble, whereas the columns of the lower level are of unadorned brick.

South of Badia, at Canda, is Scamozzi's Villa Nani Mocenigo (1580–4). Two bays flank either side of a three-bay loggia, above which is an attic storey surmounted by urns. Two broad flights of steps rise to the loggia from the shallow front garden, which is as unkempt as the villa itself. From Canda drive north-west towards the small town of Villa Bartolomea. You'll pass through the Valli Grandi Veronesi, an expansive region of canals and large brick farms and granaries reminiscent of the region north-east of Venice. On Sundays the canals that cross these bleak agricultural flatlands are lined with hundreds of fishermen; either the fish are abundant or the fishermen very optimistic.

At Villa Bartolomea the slender romanesque campanile is dwarfed by the grand but dull nineteenth-century church, set at the far end of a broad avenue lined with public buildings that seem somewhat overblown for this modest town. Legnago, to the north-west, was established in Roman times, but little remains to demonstrate the strategic importance of this town on the Adige. Opposite the church, with its unfinished brick west front, is a rounded medieval tower, also of brick, part of the former fortifications. The otherwise dull church contains in a south chapel a fourteenth-century polychrome *Pietà* of great poignancy. From Legnago a swift drive to the west brings you to Cerea, where the parish church has a romanesque campanile. There is a more interesting romanesque structure in the church of San Zeno at the northern end of town; unfortunately, to get to the entrance of the church you must first submit to being eaten alive by a boisterous hound. Behind the church, about a mile away but concealed by a copse, is the grandiose Villa Bertele, set in a spacious park.

Continue westwards to Sanguinetto. In the town square a bridge crosses to the moated castle, passing through a slender fortified brick gateway which leads into a mostly medieval courtyard, though there are many later additions. Some bays remain of an elegant cloister, and a few renaissance doorways survive. From here return to Legnago and Montagnana, and head north-west to Pressana. Next to the modern church is the sixteenth-century Villa Grimani, a most agreeable building with its arcaded loggia, low flanking towers and well-stocked garden. Along the road to Caselle is the weird Villa Querini-Stampalia, with battlemented gables at either end. Tucked against the garden wall is what might be a romanesque chapel.

The elaborate Lombard façade of the Sanctuary of the Madonna dei Miracoli near Lonigo.

At Cologna Veneta, to the north-west, the Castello del Capitaniato has been rebuilt in neo-gothic style, but the Scaliger Torre Civica survives. Next to the tower is the Palazzo di Città with its lofty arcades and handsome capitals. From here drive north-east to Orgiano, where you'll find Villa Fracanzan Piovene (1710). An exceptionally high, almost church-like façade is matched in grandeur by an agricultural wing with immense rusticated arcades. On the ground floor are splendid kitchens, still equipped with old copper utensils and a trough-like red marble sink. The rooms have remarkably ugly stone vaulting. On the *piano nobile* is a cavernous ballroom, from which the loggia overlooks the walled grounds. Above the loggia is an equally tall baroque attic storey.

Lonigo, to the north-west, is overlooked by Scamozzi's hilltop Villa La Rocca Pisana (1576), a stylish design clearly modelled on La Rotonda. In the town centre are some medieval towers and the Palazzo Pisani of 1557. With its daring double staircase (an eighteenth-century addition) and wall cartouches, this is a most lively building, so it is all the more surprising that the architect is unknown. Three kilometres south on the Cologna road is Palladio's Villa Pisani Ferri, begun in the 1540s, with its rusticated portico and low flanking towers. The agricultural wings that completed the design were demolished long ago.

Drive west to San Bonifacio. Outside the town the church of San Pietro Apostolo, close to the *autostrada*, is one of the most ancient in the Veneto, dating originally from the eighth century, though much rebuilt. The square, heavy campanile with its spacious gothic belfry, its conical roof and its plain west façade give little indication of the beauty within. The nave and aisles are separated by rounded arcades resting on a whole catalogue of capitals, mostly of byzantine and romanesque origin. The south aisle has slightly faded fourteenth-century frescoes of the life of St Benedict of Nursia, in which the figures and narrative are somewhat overshadowed by the architectural detail in which the unknown artist evidently delighted. Within the raised rounded apse is a fifteenth-century stone altar-piece, and the choir stalls are of good quality. The crypt has crude byzantine capitals, and frescoes in ruinous condition. Eight baroque statues with cornucopias stand on pedestals in the nave and choir; although out of character with the rest of the church, they are vigorously carved.

From San Bonifacio drive towards Verona, bearing south to Zevio at Caldierino. Zevio is of Roman origin. Today its finest feature is its vast central piazza. Here are located the rebuilt and trivialized moated castle, set in pretty grounds, and the nineteenth-century church, adjoining which is a very delicate pink marble renaissance gateway.

Head north, following signs for Vago. Immediately after crossing the *autostrada*, turn left and you'll see the church of San Giacomo on a hilltop two kilometres away. This fine brick gothic church has a broad five-bay façade, mostly incomplete, but it is the lofty apse, with its typically Veronese alternating bands of brick and tufa and interlaced blind arcading beneath the cornice, that is most striking. The surrounding gardens and terraces make the hilltop church a popular local excursion. Unfortunately the interior, with its frescoes by Altichiero, is only accessible during mass, the very time when tourism is discouraged.

Drive north-east to Illasi. In the village centre is the broad E-shaped Villa Carlotti (1735) by Alberto Pompei. Four Doric columns support the pediment, topped, like the balustrades over the side bays, with statues. At right angles to the villa are domestic wings and arcades with stocky towers. A few blocks behind this villa is a contemporaneous villa designed by G. B. Pozzo. The central block is filled with tall windows, and the arcaded barchesses are almost as impressive. Unlike so many eighteenth-century villas, this one has a memorably individual design. Above the village the ruined castle perches on a lovely hill filled with vines. olive groves, cypresses and, in spring, fugitive irises.

From Illasi head south to the walled town of Soave, gripped by its twenty-four towers. The best grapes of

On the slopes behind Soave are the best vineyards used to produce this famous white wine.

the famous wine to which the town lends its name are grown in the hills just behind it. Overproductive vines on the valley floor tend to produce the insipid stuff that characterizes most Soave production. No one has ever claimed that Garganega, the principal grape variety planted in Soave, is a noble grape, but in the hands of a scrupulous winemaker it can produce delicious fresh wines. Roberto Anselmi is the most fanatical of the local producers, and horrified his family by reducing substantially the quantity of wine produced by his firm in order to increase the quality. He has made radical changes in the vineyards, all of which are up· in the hills, in order to increase the concentration of fruit and flavour in his grapes. Some of his Soave is intended to be drunk when young; another bottling is stored for some time in new oak, giving the wine a richer, firmer structure that benefits from a few years in bottle. He also produces a traditional wine called Recioto: selected bunches are dried on mats in a well-ventilated loft for a few months and then pressed and vinified in small oak casks. The dried grapes have a much greater concentration of sugar and acidity than freshly picked fruit, and the result is a sweet, oaky wine that is at the same time sumptuous, powerful, and elegant. The most celebrated wines in this style come from Valpolicella and are red; the version known simply as Recioto is slightly sweet – and absolutely delicious if well made – and Amarone is bone dry and formidable. Too powerful to be drunk with meals, they are called *vini di meditazione* by the Italians, who sip them after dinner. Anselmi's range shows just how versatile and admirable the Garganega grape can be in the hands of a master winemaker. Unfortunately, when one tastes the Soave made by most of his competitors, one begins to understand why Anselmi's opinion of them is unprintable.

The main street of Soave, Via Roma, leads up to the Palazzo Cavalli (1411) in the little square facing the battlemented town hall of 1375, with its gothic arcades. To the right a lane leads steeply up to the multi-level Scaliger castle. The well-furnished public rooms are sometimes open to visitors. To the left of the town hall is Via Camuzzoni. No. 3, the fifteenth-century Palazzo Pullici, doubles as the winery of Leonildo Pieropan, another of the zone's few outstanding winemakers. He bottles separately the wines from different vineyards, and also makes a fine Recioto di Soave, though in a style very different from, and arguably more traditional than, Roberto Anselmi. The road ends at another gateway, tall and complex in its fortifications.

From Soave you can make a brief excursion through the lovely vineyards of the Soave Classico zone and into the mountains by taking the road north to Montecchia, where the church of tenth-century origin, located in the upper town's cemetery, is usually locked. Continue north to San Giovanni Ilarione, where a *Madonna and Saints* by Bartolommeo Montagna graces the parish church. Just off the road to Chiampo is the thirteenth-century chapel of San Zeno, and although it too is invariably locked, the views from the churchyard are splendid.

Return to the valley and take either the main road or the *autostrada* towards Vicenza. Just west of Vicenza is the sprawling town of Montecchio Maggiore, and on its eastern edge lies Villa Cordellina, overlooked by two mostly rebuilt castles. Built in 1735 by Giorgio Massari, the well-proportioned and elegant villa has a sumptuous garden façade with a lofty portico. The estate works well as a unit, with handsome outbuildings and attractive gardens. Within the villa are frescoes by G. B. Tiepolo. Towards the town the church of San Pietro has an altar-piece in the south aisle by Giovanni Buonconsiglio. A few kilometres north of Montecchio is the hillside village of Trissino, the domain of Palladio's great patron. The eighteenth-century Villa Trissino stands within the former castle grounds, and consists of two villas, luxuriating in what is now an extensive terraced park. Many of the statues are by Orazio Marinali. Return to Montecchio and take the *autostrada* to Vicenza. Just after the exit

The Scaligeri warlords kept a firm grip on many towns of the Veneto from castles such as this one at Soave.

Even in a small town like Thiene you can find exquisite designs such as this renaissance doorway.

follow signs for the abbey of San Agostino (1322), an aiseless church with contemporary frescoes in the nave and choir, where there is a sinuous depiction of the Crucifixion. A complex early fifteenth-century polyptych by Battista da Vicenza stands behind the altar. The abbey is only a few kilometres from central Vicenza.

The interesting and topographically varied area north of Vicenza is also ideally explored using the city as a base. The first village of interest to the north is Caldogno, where the villa of that name is attributed to Palladio (1570). It has three rusticated arcades, and the interior has contemporary frescoes. An improbable number of villas around Vicenza are attributed to Palladio, but this particular identification at least seems plausible. A small but striking feature is the lozenge-shaped opening in the pediment. Just north-east of Caldogno, at Vivaro, is the imposing Villa Da Porto Del Conte; its core is probably sixteenth-century

but there are many later additions. Here the most arresting feature is the Ionic colonnade of the deep portico. Between here and Dueville is Villa Da Porto Casarotto, a pompous and coarsely detailed work by Calderari (1770). In the centre of Dueville the town hall is the former Villa Monza, a rather pinched structure with an arcade of double columns and projecting central bays. The concentration of villas, not all of which are architectural masterpieces by any means, makes it possible to understand how the Veneto and Friuli between them can be dotted with literally thousands of villas that are anything from five to two centuries old. Unlike the equally numerous châteaux of France, they rarely have any defensive function, but are primarily farms and working estates where agricultural productivity can be combined with good living.

At Villaverla, just north of Dueville, the town hall occupies Scamozzi's broad, stately but – thanks to rusticated lower storeys – rather grim Villa Verlato. Just beyond, on the Thiene road, is Villa Ghellini, built by Antonio Pizzocaro in 1664–79. A taller version of Villa Verlato, this is unfinished and remains a shell. It is nonetheless imposing, with an impressive obelisked gateway too.

Thiene itself is a pleasant town with a sprinkling of older houses in its centre. The *duomo* is a grand but bland seventeenth-century building, strictly classical in style. The best feature of the interior is the nave's sumptuous coffered ceiling, richly frescoed in gloomy tones. The more recent artist who decorated the modern dome evidently had a penchant for dramatic scenes involving well-muscled men, and his work has some entertainment value. Opposite the *duomo* is the church of Santo Rosario, begun in the fourteenth century but much added to subsequently. Alongside the church, statues of St Peter and St Paul, originally from the *duomo* façade, stand on ground-level pedestals. The interior is enriched with dazzling rococo altar-pieces and aisle ceilings. Angels fling themselves joyously all over the domed roof of the choir; some of the plasterwork is painted a strident lilac, a bizarre choice of colour but peculiarly successful. This riotous ornament overshadows the many frescoes in the church, but the painting above the altar, the *Madonna of the Rosary* (1590) signed by Mateo Grazioli, is of good quality. There is also a finely carved walnut font cover of 1664. This is certainly one of the liveliest churches in the northern Veneto.

Walk beneath the lofty brick campanile next to the church and you will enter a small piazza. Turn left on to the Corso Garibaldi and after about 100 m you will come to extensive castellated walls that surround the Villa da Porto-Colleoni (1490), more a castle than a villa, with its symbolic castellations on both wings of the structure. The windows, especially the central five-bay opening, are carved in an often sumptuous late Venetian-gothic style. Opposite the entrance gate stands the contemporary chapel of the Nativity in a similar style. There are weathered busts in the roundels of the ogee gable; the south portal is also carved. Next to this chapel is the Casetta Rossa, a chunky little house with a finely carved renaissance portal and an elaborate roof. The villa itself is open to the public and has frescoes by Zelotti and other sixteenth-century painters, as well as a collection of furniture. (Incidentally, half-way down the Corso there is a splendid art nouveau house with leafy ironwork along the balconies – not at all what you expect to find in this corner of Italy.)

Directly west of Thiene is Schio, a textile town cupped within the foothills of the mountains that lie between the Vicenza plain and the Dolomites. The eighteenth-century *duomo* is set dramatically on a white marble balustraded terrace. The lumpish classical portico with its heavy Corinthian columns is a later addition, as is the grand double staircase connecting the terrace with the piazza below. One would have expected the terrace to overlook the plain, but, on the contrary, it faces the wooded hills behind the town. Directly opposite is the slender tower of the *castello*. Of the original castle nothing remains, and the church-like building and tower that now exist are essentially a reconstruction. The *castello* is situated in a small shady park that tops a hillock and keeps the bustle of the town at bay. It's an enjoyable place to sit with a book for half an hour.

Most gothic façades in the Veneto are built of brick, but not all are as elegant as this chapel in Thiene.

The fifteenth-century church of San Francesco, with its fine gothic campanile, is close to the road to Asiago on the northern edge of town. The interior is apparently adorned with frescoes and early sixteenth-century choir stalls, but I have never found the church open. Just beyond it on the Asiago road is a large war memorial and cemetery in the form of a cloister. This is one of many reminders in this region of the casualties suffered by, among others less conspicuously memorialized, the Italians and Austro-Hungarians between 1915 and 1918.

To explore the mountains behind Schio, take the road to Valli del Pasubio, and there turn left to Recoaro. The village of Staro has a church of 1695 with an attractive west front. Cross Passo Xon, from which there are good views of the Valdastico mountains. Hairpin bends take you down to the pleasant little spa of Recoaro. From here a very steep road climbs to the

Left Vernacular statuary outside the neo-classical cathedral at Schio.

Above The soaring pinnacles of Enego, the most easterly town on the plateau of the *Sette Comuni*.

165

Campogrosso pass (1457 m), but the route is subject to landslides and is not always open. Travelling the minor roads in this region is a game of chance. You are quite likely to share my experience and find roads unexpectedly closed, necessitating a laborious round trip. Although this area can't compete with the splendours of the Dolomites, it is nonetheless attractive and far less crowded than the better known mountains to the north.

To visit the Valdastico region itself, take the Asiago road from Schio and follow signs for Arsiero, which is due north of Schio but cannot be reached directly because a mountain intervenes. From Arsiero drive up the Valdastico valley – not an especially exciting journey. You can cross the bridge at San Pietro, a somewhat drab village redeemed by its location beneath cliffs, and turn left immediately beyond the church. This steep road will take you to Rotzo, but the route is recommended only to devotees of single-track roads. More pusillanimous travellers should watch for signs for Rotzo several kilometres before San Pietro. The road climbs not up to a pass, but to a large plateau on which a number of towns and villages are situated, all at a height of about 1000 m. These are known as the *Sette Comuni* ('Seven Communities'). The first one you reach is Castelletto; near the village excavations have uncovered a Gallic site and altar. Some of the towns on this delightfully airy and verdant plateau are small resorts, such as Roana and Asiago. The landscape is not dramatic, but has great breadth and gentleness, with rolling grassy hills divided by stone terraces and topped with pine forests.

Asiago strikes me as wonderfully old-fashioned, with its hip-roofed houses and hotels – mostly built after the destruction wreaked during World War I – painted rather faded shades of pink and buff. Unlike many of the villages around Schio and Arsiero, these plateau communities are neat and well maintained. In the centre of Asiago is the *duomo*, a pink marble edifice completed in 1915. Despite the date, its architectural language is identical to that of all the countless neoclassical basilica-type churches strewn throughout this part of the Veneto. Yet it is worth visiting the cathedral to see, behind the altar, a refined *Madonna and Child* by Francesco Bassano the Elder. On the eastern edge of town is the Sacrario Militare, a huge arched memorial to the tens of thousands of soldiers who died here. Return to Schio by following signs for Vicenza. About three kilometres out of Asiago, at Canove, a museum commemorates the battles of 1915–18. The road descends from the plateau, elegantly navigating ten hairpin bends, from which there are ample views of the plain below.

A few kilometres to the east after the descent is the village of Lugo, north-east of Thiene. Should you approach from Thiene, you will see up on the hillside the portico of the splendid Villa Piovene-Porto Godi (Piovene for short). As you drive towards it up the winding road, you will pass a less conspicuous villa, Villa Godi-Malinveni (Godi for short). This singularly austere house, with no exterior ornament at all and its projecting side blocks, was the first villa designed by Palladio and was probably completed by about 1540. A livelier touch is displayed on the terraces, which are watched over by a gang of statues. Villa Piovene is much more enjoyable, although the most exuberant features – the fine Ionic portico, the splendid flight of steps that dashes from gate to portico, the flamboyant gateway with its statues and urns – are later additions. Only the garden, with its eighteenth-century grottoes, is open to the public.

Drive down the main Thiene-Bassano road and head for Bassano, turning right before the town for Marostica. Visible from afar are the defensive walls and towers climbing two sides of a hill to meet at the Castello Superiore, a Scaliger construction, on the summit. The small town below is also fiercely defended by its own walls and towers. From 1311 to 1386 the Scaligeri controlled the town and gave it its present layout; after a brief period of Visconti rule, the Venetians took over Marostica in 1404. The main square is dominated by the Castello Inferiore, now the

Frescoes beneath the loggia of one of Palladio's earliest works, the Villa Godi-Malinveni at Lugo.

Above **The immaculate piazza at Marostica, where every two years a medieval chess game is re-enacted.**

Right **A swooping baroque staircase leads up to the Villa Rossini near Marostica.**

Powerful colonnades lead into the park at Villa Contarini-Simes.

A caryatid scratches his laden head on the façade of the Villa Contarini-Simes at Piazzola.

town hall, a splendid battlemented rectangle facing both the piazza and the once hostile world outside the walls. Marostica attains momentary celebrity every two years, when a game of chess, once played between two citizens in 1454 to decide who would win the *podestà*'s daughter in marriage, is re-enacted, an event full of pageantry and music that gives occupation to five hundred men, women, and children of the town. The paving of the square is permanently laid out in chess squares in readiness. The slopes just beyond the town, heading towards the plateau around Asiago, are filled not only with olive groves but with trees bearing the region's best-known crop, cherries.

Follow signs for Nove, then Cartigliano, where, near the centre, stands the Villa Morosini-Cappello. The ground floor brick arcades and first-floor colonnades swoop right round the building. This is a vigorous composition of the late sixteenth century by, it's thought, Francesco Zamberlan. In the south chapel of

the parish church is a sadly damaged altar-piece by Bartolommeo Montagna, and a sparingly painted fresco cycle of 1575 by Jacopo Bassano and his son Francesco. Just east of here is Ca' Donfin. If many Veneto villas are structurally simple, whatever the sophistication of their decorative schemes, this cannot be said of this late seventeenth-century villa. The architect is unknown. The façade gives more prominence to the attic storey than is usual, and the central bays are toped by a rounded pediment. The villa is tall in relation to its width, and backs onto a park well stocked with mature trees.

From here take the road south to Cittadella. This small town is entirely surrounded by a wall almost two kilometres in length, watched over by thirty-two towers, all of which date from the 1220s and are remarkably well preserved. They were built to protect the town from attacks from the north, and served their purpose well until Can Francesco Scaligeri captured the town, which then fell into Paduan hands from 1321 to 1405. Thereafter Cittadella became a Venetian outpost. During the Middle Ages, the entire province of Padua was scattered with about seventy castles and fortified towns. Today the best preserved are Montagnana and Cittadella. The gateways are superb and deep, and must have been thoroughly discouraging to anyone tempted to penetrate them. Inside, however, is one of the least interesting of the walled towns of the Veneto. The cathedral is a cold neo-classical job by Ottavio Scamozzi and few of the houses are of much interest.

South of Cittadella is Piazzola sul Brenta, the site of one of the most magnificent of the Veneto villas, Villa Contarini-Simes. Far more of a palace than a villa, it has been attributed by some to Palladio, though what is visible today is essentially a seventeenth-century baroque *palazzo*. The wings were added at that time, and the villa is linked to the town by arcades that leap the road and develop into a colonnade that half encircles a large piazza. You can visit an endless series of rooms: some frescoed with large romping figures in pastoral landscapes, an immense gallery inlaid with shells, other rooms decorated with mosaics or Etruscan motifs or tiles. Upstairs are a vast and half-empty library, a galleried music room, stuccoed drawing rooms and bedrooms, cursorily adorned with poor furniture and worse paintings, and a stuffed bird collection. The interior is in fairly awful taste, but it does give one an idea of the vast scale on which the Italian nobility once lived.

From here head west towards Vicenza. Palladio aficionados might want to make a slight detour to the north to Quinto. Here the town hall is the former Villa Thiene of Palladio, built in 1546. Sadly it now bears little relation to his published designs. It lacks, shall we say, amiability. The road front is dominated by a vast pediment, added during the last century, that covers the width of the villa. Nor is the aesthetic aspect improved by boarded-up windows and ghastly modern modifications to the less oppressive rear façade. It seems odd that a work by so major an architect should have been given such shoddy treatment over the years.

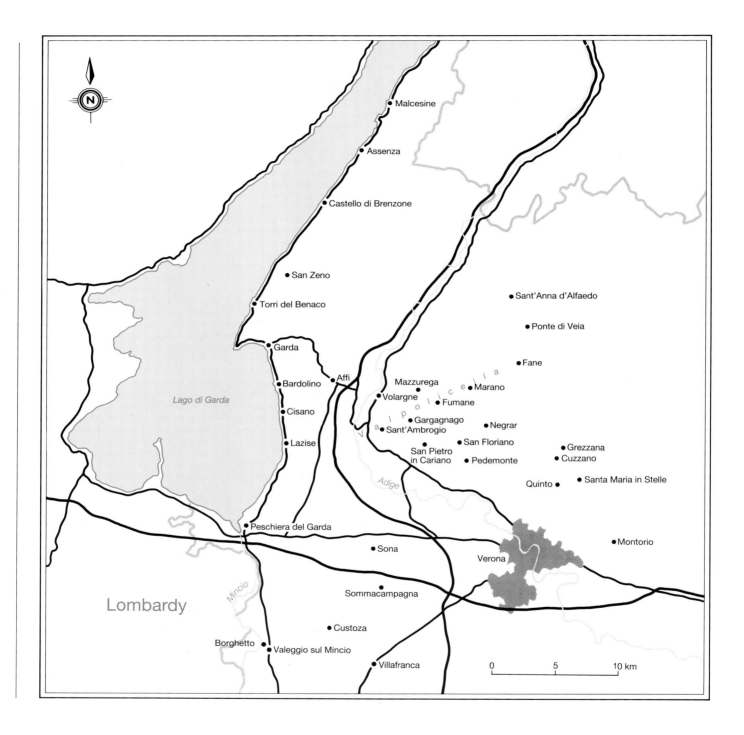

Malcesine

Assenza

Castello di Brenzone

San Zeno

Torri del Benaco

Sant'Anna d'Alfaedo

Ponte di Veia

Fane

Garda

Affi

Mazzurega

Marano

Bardolino

Volargne

Fumane

Lago di Garda

Cisano

Gargagnago

Negrar

Sant'Ambrogio

Lazise

San Floriano

Grezzana

San Pietro
in Cariano

Pedemonte

Cuzzano

Adige

Quinto

Santa Maria in Stelle

Peschiera del Garda

Montorio

Sona

Verona

Sommacampagna

Mincio

Lombardy

Custoza

Borghetto

Valeggio sul Mincio

Villafranca

Valpolicella

0   5   10 km

5
Verona and Lake Garda

Verona — Villafranca — Peschiera del Garda — Garda —

Malcesine — Valpolicella

Of all the cities of the Veneto, other than Venice itself, Verona has the firmest grip on my affections. It has a style, an integrity, a panache, and a grandeur of its own, integrating its various functions – trade centre, cultural centre, industrial manufacture, tourist venue – with remarkable success. True, the traffic can be even more tangled than is usual in most Italian towns, and the industrial outskirts have an ugliness and confusion reminiscent of Naples, but these are not the lingering impressions with which one leaves Verona.

You have only to glance at the Roman amphitheatre, the Arena, to realize that this has long been a very important town. The Romans colonized it in 89 BC, and the city prospered at the hub of the major trade routes leading from Italy to the Alps and beyond. Verona fell, successively, into the hands of Ostrogoths and Lombards before its capture by Charlemagne in 774. Charlemagne's offspring built palaces in the city, confirming its prestige and centrality. Verona became a free commune early in the twelfth century, and was a leading player in the league that saw off the hostile forces of Holy Roman Emperor Frederick Barbarossa later that century. The ubiquitous tyrant Ezzelino III da Romano ruled the city until 1259, when a local militia chief, Mastino I della Scala, took control of Verona and began what was to become the dynastic rule of the Scaligeri. Power tempered the Scaligeri,

who sought and gained demonstrable public support for what was essentially a tyranny and who had the confidence to contribute in a major way to the cultural splendour of the city. Dante was welcomed here in 1304 as an exile from Florence, and Ghibelline exiles from Tuscany found refuge in Verona during the rule of the most illustrious of the Scaligeri, Can Francesco, more familiarly known as Cangrande I. During his reign from 1311 to 1329, he gathered within his embrace Vicenza and Belluno and, in the year before his death, Padua, which brought the Scaligeri into severe conflict not only with Venice, but with other centres of power such as Milan and Florence. They were ultimately to prove the victors.

Scaliger rule ended in 1387, and Verona had to submit to another selection of familiar warlords from the Visconti and Carraresi dynasties, until in 1405, together with most of the other major cities of the Veneto, it came under lasting Venetian control. This ended only with the French occupation of the city in 1796, an unhappy and destructive period for Verona, since Napoleon responded to uprisings with ferocity and greed. In 1814 the Austrians took control and remained until the incorporation of Verona into the new kingdom of Italy in 1866.

Most of the old city is contained within the embrace of the meandering Adige, and many, though by no

173

means all, of Verona's major monuments are concentrated within this loop. The renewal of the fortifications in the mid sixteenth century gave the city an approximation of a formal entrance through the gate called Porta Nuova, now close to the railway station. From here a broad boulevard, Corso Porta Nuova, leads to the remains of the more ancient medieval walls that once enclosed the heart of the city. Porta Nuova itself, like all the renaissance fortifications, is the work of Michele Sammicheli (1484–1559), a local architect whose prolific activities contributed greatly not only to the beauty of Verona but to the architectural legacy of the Veneto as a whole. He studied in Rome and was greatly influenced by Michelangelo. He returned to Verona in 1527 and by the time he died had designed four major palaces, as well as numerous churches and fortifications. Employed by the Venetian Republic, he travelled widely and is known to have visited some of the Mediterranean islands with extant Greek temples and ruins. Thus it is probable that Sammicheli was one of the few great architects of the Renaissance who had been able to study such models at first hand.

Porta Nuova now functions as a traffic island, and it is debatable whether it is worth braving the swirl of cars and buses to inspect at close quarters this somewhat confused mass of brick and stone. Sammicheli was in charge of the maintenance and modernization of Verona's fortifications for over thirty years, and students of military architecture place both Porta Nuova and Porta San Giorgio, also by Sammicheli, as among the greatest renaissance gateways in all of Italy.

Corso Porto Nuova is the city's major commercial street; a few older *palazzi* and churches are preserved, though none is of especial interest. The first road to the right, Via Battisti, leads to the attractive romanesque church of the Trinità. You enter the church through a kind of half-cloistered atrium, which contains a pink marble tomb of 1421. The interior, like so many in Verona, has been classicized, although a few fifteenth-century frescoes remain in place.

The Corso ends at the Portoni della Brà, two lofty castellated arches attached on one side to a single tall tower. This structure of 1389 was at one time linked to Castelvecchio, the riverside fortress of the Scaligeri. Just as you pass through the gate, you will see on your left the entrance to the oldest lapidary museum in Europe, which is well worth a visit. The Portoni lead into the immense Piazza Brà, a square large enough to contain at the far end the third largest extant Roman amphitheatre and still have room to spare for a small park in the centre. On the right is the hefty seventeenth-century *palazzo* of the Gran Guardia, with its mighty rusticated arcades. Beyond the Gran Guardia are further vestiges of the medieval city walls, and then the nineteenth-century Palazzo Municipale. The piazza is civilized by the presence of the gently curving Liston, an eighteenth-century promenade overlooked by a varied assortment of renaissance *palazzi* and houses. The Liston is arcaded and broad enough to accommodate the tables of the many cafés and restaurants here.

The Arena has been much restored but remains undeniably impressive. Charles Dickens was beguiled completely, finding the amphitheatre 'so well preserved and carefully maintained, that every row of seats is there, unbroken'. The best way to experience the Arena is simply to clamber up the banks of seating, hauling yourself up from ancient stone to ancient stone. The Arena was built in the first century AD and can seat 22,000 spectators. Of the outer wall only four arches remain, the rest having succumbed to various earthquakes, but their sheer height renders them conspicuous. In 1913 a performance of *Aida* within the Arena sparked a notion that has since become one of Italy's great cultural success stories, and the opera season here thrives through the summer months. As one would expect, the staples of the season are the major Verdi operas, such as *Aida* and *La Traviata*, well suited to performance in the vast spaces of the Arena beneath a star-filled summer sky.

The Arena thrives in winter too, as part of the city's Christmas festivities. Every December a 60 m steel arch

In Verona you are never far from the River Adige, which curves through the old city.

comes springing out of the Arena into the piazza, where it bursts at ground level into a complex star with thirty-two points. One year I watched as lorries trundled into the Arena with no fewer than two million tin cans that had once contained beer and soft drinks. On the floor of the amphitheatre, a precise replica of the Arena itself was being constructed out of this debris. The outer walls and seats showed the enormous share of the market commanded by the Coca-Cola company, while the inner walls gave Pepsi and Fanta and Heineken a look in too. Not only was money raised for charity, but it was also great fun, and even elderly Veronese ladies were seen clambering to the top of the Arena and gasping with delight.

Behind the Arena from the Portoni you can see the choir of San Nicolò. Its main entrance has a mighty neo-classical façade with tall Ionic half-columns supporting the pediment. Curiously, this façade was tacked on after World War II; it formerly belonged to the church of San Sebastiano, which was destroyed in 1945. If you stand back, the superimposition becomes obvious yet remains ingenious.

Return to the piazza and turn right. You'll come in a few yards to Via Mazzini (also known as Via Nuova), a pedestrianized lane that prolongs the Liston. Lined with smart clothes shops, it is the haunt of Verona's inexhaustible supply of chic women of all ages. When you come to Via Scala, turn right. The block is filled with the bays of a finely proportioned eighteenth-century *palazzo*, now the Hotel Accademia. Just beyond the *palazzo* is the early fourteenth-century church of Santa Maria della Scala. The church sustained serious bomb damage in 1945 and has been skilfully rebuilt, and many works of art, notably a pretty series of fifteenth-century frescoes, have been preserved. On the south wall is the fine early renaissance tomb of Paolo Filippo Guantieri (1430), attributed to Antonio da Mestre. The composition of the heavily canopied and frescoed monument is grand but leaden, but there is a tiny tabernacle beneath, framed with carvings of saints, that has more lightness of touch.

Return to Via Mazzini. In another few metres you will pass on your left a fine *palazzo* with an elegant renaissance portal. At the end of Via Mazzini, turn right on to Via Cappello, which soon brings you to the austere gothic façade of the Casa di Giulietta – Juliet's House. The story of Romeo and Juliet was a sixteenth-century invention – there is no historical evidence to suggest that the Capulet and Montecchi clans were anything other than good friends – but it may have ensured the preservation of one of Verona's earliest mansions. Dickens described the building as 'a most miserable little inn' in the 1840s, and it has not recovered much cheerfulness since. The aspect from the courtyard is the most pleasurable, showing fine trefoiled windows and, of course, the famous balcony. But the interior is a grave disappointment. Some of the rooms have painted walls, mostly vandalized by lovers so assiduous that they have scratched the names of their *innamorati* all the way through to the plaster beneath. On the top floor the wooden ceilings are prettily if tepidly painted, but the house as a whole is woefully lacking in character and furnishings. There are better ways to spend a few thousand lire. Nor is it worth while to traipse half-way across Verona to visit the alleged tomb of the alleged Juliet: one empty sarcophagus is much like another.

The best time, or perhaps the worst, to visit these pedestrian enclaves is in the early evening, when, it seems, every Veronese is out on the street. Just as there is traffic gridlock on the boulevards, so there is human gridlock on Via Mazzini. Old women in fur coats, young women in stylish capes, staid couples, all stroll arm in arm, making any swift passage impossible. Clumps of Veronese, joyfully greeting their friends, block the street. Flower sellers and musicians give further pretexts for delay. Yet it is hard to resent all this activity, for it shows the city at its most warm and agreeable, taking on the familiarity of an immense village.

The sixteenth-century frescoes bring life and colour to the Case Mazzanti overlooking Verona's Piazza delle Erbe.

The grand renaissance staircase within the courtyard of the Palazzo della Ragione.

From Juliet's House return down Via Cappello until you enter Piazza delle Erbe, once the site of the Roman forum. The bustle of the market – clothes, fast food stalls, even hamsters and canaries – can obscure the splendours of the piazza, but it is worth lingering, for there is much to see. The square is well furnished: there's a column of pink marble with a carved lantern of indifferent quality, two fountains, one of them medieval, and a sixteenth-century column bearing the winged lion of St Mark. Half-way up the left side of the piazza looms the heavily restored Casa dei Mercanti. Its style and its arcades, rather than its materials or details, allude to its fourteenth-century origins. In the far corner of the piazza is tucked the slender battle-mented Torre Gardello of 1370, and next to it the five bays of the Palazzo Maffei (1668). This is a gorgeous building, with layer piled upon layer of vigorously carved stonework. Above the top storey is a cornice ornamented with cartouches, then a balustrade, and on top of that six statues surveying the square. It's a theatrical composition, striking a most welcome note after the austerity of the Arena and the fortifications. On the right side of the piazza are the broad Case Mazzanti, a row of heavily eaved houses, all with painted walls; these sixteenth-century frescoes are faded but still pleasantly colourful, and the verdant roof terraces and window boxes add to the cheer. You can walk behind the houses into Via Mazzanti, from where the view is equally picturesque. At the beginning of this lane stands a massive renaissance marble well.

The remainder of this side of the square is filled with the intimidating bulk of the Palazzo della Ragione. From the top of its immense medieval campanile, the Torre dei Lamberti, there are splendid views of the city below. At the other end of the façade is the grim brick pile of the Torre delle Carceri, but the rest of the piazza side of the *palazzo* was rebuilt, clumsily, during the last century. The courtyard, with its lofty arcades on rounded arches, shows its romanesque origins. The walls, like the lower stages of the Torre dei Lamberti, are constructed from alternating bands of stone and brick, a hallmark of the Veronese style. A broad flight of steps, built of pink marble and supported on four fifteenth-century arches of irregular size and shape, rises to the upper floor.

You can stroll from the courtyard or from Piazza delle Erbe into the adjoining Piazza dei Signori. A statue of Dante gazes towards the lane that bears his name and on to the arch that links the Palazzo della Ragione with the massive fourteenth-century brick tower of the Tribunale (or Palazzo del Capitano), originally a Scaligeri palace and subsequently the law courts. Enter the Tribunale through Sammicheli's renaissance portal – one of many such portals in the piazza – and you will find yourself in the Cortile del Tribunale. Straight ahead is the wildly brutalist gateway, embellished with martial emblems, designed

A grim-faced statue of Dante surveys the Piazza dei Signori in Verona.

by Miglioranzi in 1687. By peering through the large glass cover over the pink marble well in the Cortile you can glimpse Roman paving some metres below. (There is more of the same in Via Dante.) Return to Piazza dei Signori, where you will now be facing the skilfully carved, pilastered, frescoed, and statued Loggia del Consiglio, the city council building completed in 1493, perfectly proportioned and very elegant. Between the Loggia and the Tribunale is the much restored, battlemented Prefettura, another former Scaligeri stronghold, its crisp renaissance portal surmounted by a relief portraying the winged lion of Venice.

Not far from these somewhat grim municipal palaces is an area much frequented by students and soldiers, many of whom patronize the simple, noisy *trattorie* near the Piazza Indipendenza. I enjoyed eating there – when I could find a space. The food was inexpensive and unsophisticated, but tasty and well cooked, and the atmosphere invariably cheerful. I once had to share a table with a toothless crone adorned with a hairnet, who insisted, in the course of her mostly incomprehensible discourse, on sharing with me much of the food on her plate. She put away half a litre of wine in no time at all, and we had a splendid time. True, the food is better at the sumptuous Il Desco restaurant (and ten times the price), but I found these boisterous *trattorie* thoroughly enjoyable, and far better value than the bland and predictable tourist traps along Corso Porta Nuova and around Piazza Brà.

The passage between the Tribunale and Prefettura leads to the Scaliger tombs and the small romanesque church of Santa Maria Antica. The capitals are unornamented and the church is refreshingly bereft of baroque altar-pieces. Services here attract a loyal congregation of very old ladies, all identically dressed, who seem to roam in packs moving from mass to mass in the old city. Opposite the church is the entrance to the courtyard of the Prefettura, and its arcaded sections have painted wooden roofs and walls.

Above the entrance to the church is the tomb of Cangrande himself, by Bonino da Campione (*fl*.1357–75). It has a luxurious trefoiled canopy and an equestrian statue, a copy of the original now displayed

in the Castelvecchio, on the very top. All the other Scaliger tombs are enclosed in an adjoining courtyard, which is surrounded by a two-metre-high pink marble wall, topped with a splendid fourteenth-century ironwork grille to the same height. Since one of the tombs (that of Mastino II della Scala, who died in 1351) was damaged as a consequence of the 1976 earthquake in the Friuli, there is no direct access to the courtyard while repairs slowly continue. The only easily visible tomb is the spectacular one, also by Bonino, of Cansignorio Scaliger, who died in 1375. It's an exuberant piece of work, with the tomb mounted on a six-sided pedestal, which is elaborately canopied with gables filled with statues and an equestrian statue atop it all. The pedestal and tomb are surrounded by six canopied statues mounted on tall square columns, some of which double as wallposts.

From the tombs walk down Vicolo Cavalletto to Corso Santa Anastasia. Turn right and you will soon see the harsh brick façade of the church of Santa Anastasia itself, for it remains incomplete with all its ribs still showing. (Shortly before you reach the church piazza, an archway on the left leads to Palazzo Forti. Napoleon stayed here in 1796–7 and in more recent times the palace has been housing Verona's modern Italian art collection and a museum celebrating the reunification of Italy, the Risorgimento.) The reliefs of 1522 around the portal of Santa Anastasia have been badly mutilated but the ornamented pink marble frames that enclosed the panels are reasonably intact, as are the fine early fourteenth-century carvings along the lintel. You enter the church through massive wooden doors. The water stoups attached to the first piers of the nave are supported on realistically carved caryatids known as *i gobbi* (hunchbacks); the one on the left took his bow in 1495, the other a century later.

The church, the largest in Verona, has an exceptionally broad nave, and the piers are so widely spaced that

Renaissance and medieval palaces side by side in Verona's Piazza dei Signori.

there is little division spatially between nave and aisles. Although the church, a Dominican foundation, was built over many centuries and not completed until 1481, it has remarkable unity of style and is one of the major gothic edifices in the Veneto. The first chapel of the south aisle consists of the severe monument to Giano Fregoso by Danese Cattaneo (1565). It has many admirers, among them Vasari, but I find its classicism very cold. Beyond the fourth chapel and on the nearby piers are fourteenth-century frescoes of considerable refinement. The last chapel in the aisle contains the tomb of Gianesello da Folgaria, who died in 1424; this splendid monument is carved with an Entombment by Bartolomeo Giolfino. In the south transept stands a gothic tomb and a large clumsy renaissance altar-piece redeemed by the fine *Madonna and Saints* (1512) by Girolamo dai Libri (1474–1555).

There are five absidal chapels. Furthest to the right is the Cappella Cavalli with admirable frescoes by Altichiero, depicting the saint doing some special pleading on behalf of the Cavalli family. The frescoes are packed with fine architectural detail. The tomb and sloping effigy of Federico Cavalli are shaded by a gothic arch, and within the lunette is a fine fresco by Stefano da Zevio (1375–1451). The neighbouring chapel, Cappella Pellegrini, is packed to the roof with twenty-four terracotta reliefs (1435) by Michele da Firenze, surely an *embarras de richesse*. The chapel also contains two fourteenth-century tombs, both adorned with excellent frescoes; those on the left are by Altichiero. Note too the graceful and dignified sixteenth-century frescoes of saints by Michele da Verona on the pilasters by the chapel entrance; here too the architectural motifs are beautifully depicted.

The choir has grand but rather stiff fourteenth-century frescoes of the Last Judgment that came to light only in 1942. Opposite them is the splendid early fifteenth-century tomb of the *condottiere* Cortesia Serego, and above it an equestrian statue of the

gentleman rides away from us. The tomb, attributed to Nanni di Bartolo (*fl.*1419–51), is revealed to the spectator by two soldiers pulling aside heavy curtains, and the entire composition is framed within a gigantic cartouche. To the left of the choir is the Lavagnoli chapel, also with sumptuous and meticulous fifteenth-century frescoes.

From the transept a door leads into the Cappella Giusti, completed in 1453. It's a shabby room at first glance, but closer inspection brings rewards. The furnishings include an altar-piece by Felice Brusasorci (1546–1605), sombre late fifteenth-century choir stalls and a massive lectern, a small quantity of medieval stained glass, and, at the opposite end to the altar, Pisanello's fresco of St George and the princess. It's an extraordinary work, with only hints of colour; indeed, unilluminated, it looks like a monochrome painting. The decorative elements, the caparisoned horses and other animals, the distant towers and castles, almost overshadow the human encounter. This bizarre opulence is portrayed in the foreground, while in the distance two men hang from a gibbet. The exoticism and mysteriousness of this painting make all the other frescoes in Santa Anastasia, for all their excellence, seem tame and conventional by comparison.

Pisanello (1395–1455/6) was probably born, as his name suggests, in Pisa, but he was raised in Verona, where he was clearly influenced by Stefano da Verona and such masters of the international gothic style as Gentile da Fabriano. He was, like so many medieval masters, an itinerant artist, but he returned to Verona in 1433 to begin work on this fresco, which was not completed until 1438. It is surely one of the masterpieces of international gothic, with all the meticulously painted detail and self-conscious gorgeousness of that style. Yet there is more to the painting than opulence. In its lack of narrative coherence and its very fragility it captures the last gasp of the gothic era at its most fantastical, just moments, it would seem, before the psychological and narrative power of the renaissance styles erupted.

Return to the main church and the north aisle. The first chapel after the transept houses a very beautiful

---

Carved hunchbacks support the water stoups in the huge church of Santa Anastasia.

Left **Romanesque saints guard the main portal of Verona's *duomo*.**

Above **A vigorously carved capital from the south portal of the *duomo* in Verona.**

185

Madonna and Saints attributed to Lorenzo Veneziano. The painting radiates an intense spirituality, and puts to the shame the efficient but flashy baroque grandeur of the rest of the chapel, which was built to celebrate the victory at Lepanto. Beyond the gilt-cased organ is a lofty altar-piece with five tiers of statues on either side and numerous marble reliefs; this splendid piece was erected in 1436. The last chapel along the aisle is similarly constructed, if slightly less lofty. All this polychrome statuary may strike a crude note, but it is strong and expressive, and in fascinating contrast to the more sophisticated but less engaging Danese Cattaneo monument facing it.

On leaving the church, you'll see on the right of the piazza a canopied gothic monument to Guglielmo Castelbarco, who died in 1320. Next to it is the brick chapel of San Pietro Martire, founded in 1283 and used by the Dominicans while Santa Anastasia was being completed. Although the chapel is now secularized and functions as an art gallery, its frescoes have been preserved. These include a bizarre allegory of the Annunciation by animal-loving Giovanni Maria Falconetto, whose more illustrious achievements as an architect we have already encountered. In the Veneto his work is best represented by the loggias he built for Alvise Cornaro in Padua (p. 108). Alongside Santa Anastasia, following the embankment of the Adige, is Via Sottoriva; beneath its medieval arcades are a number of fine shops, including one of the best wine shops in the Veneto.

On leaving the piazza turn right into Via Duomo, which is lined with *palazzi*. This leads to the *duomo*, built after the earthquake of 1117 destroyed its eighth-century predecessor. Consecrated in 1187, it was gothicized in the late fifteenth century, and is dominated by its vast white campanile, crammed with cornices, balustrades, pilasters, and obelisks – the full repertory of renaissance architectural motifs. It is massive and bold, as you would expect from Sammicheli, but it is not a heart-warming sight. The bell stage is a modern addition. It is rather a relief to let the eyes descend to the simple bands of tufa and brick from which the *duomo* walls are built. The south portal is shaded by a frescoed canopy resting on columns with carved capitals and entablatures carved with animal motifs, including a representation of Jonah and the whale. Opposite the portal a canopied and seated fourteenth-century statue, badly worn, of St Peter dominates a portal of the now disused church of San Pietro in Archivolto.

The *duomo*'s south portal is a trifle compared to the much grander composition on the west façade: a two-storied structure of pink and white stone, embellished with reliefs and friezes and carved capitals. This is fifteenth-century work, whereas the doorway itself and the carvings around it date from 1140 and are mostly the work of Maestro Nicolò. The principal columns rest on the backs of two lions. The doorway is ringed with carved reliefs of animals, flowers, and a superb series of saints. Pilasters flanking the portal are embellished with statues of Charlemagne's Paladin knights, Roland and Oliver, guarding over the structure, their swords unsheathed.

Despite some grand neo-classical intrusions, the interior has retained its gothic arcades of pink marble and its vaulting. The side chapels are defined by renaissance frames: pilasters topped with statues. Begin by walking down the south aisle. The second chapel has a profusion of panels by Liberale da Verona (1445–1526) and Nicola Giolfino (1476–1555). Just beyond it is a romanesque stoup, the bowl supported on the backs of crouching caryatids. Just before you come to the organ loft you will pass beneath a fifteenth-century painted Crucifix. The organ itself is elaborately carved and gilt and is additionally adorned with painted doors. At the end of the south aisle is the superb renaissance Cappella Mazzanti, framed by brilliantly designed and carved pilasters of flesh-toned marble. This is workmanship of the very highest quality, and has been attributed to Domenico da Lugo (1508). Within the monument is the tomb of St Agatha (1353), watched over by figures of angels; along the roof of the canopy is a frieze of seven Apostles. To the right of the chapel is the tomb slab of Pope Lucius III, who died in Verona in 1185. Sammicheli's semicircular marble choir screen of 1534 seems somewhat

The canopied south portal of the *duomo* at Verona is decorated inside with frescoes.

unimaginative after the inventiveness of the Mazzanti chapel. The Crucifix and statues above the choir entrance are by Giambattista da Verona. Along the north aisle, between the second and third chapels, is a fine *Madonna and Saints* by Gian Francesco Caroto (c.1488–1555). At the west end, the Cappella Cartolari-Nichesola contains an *Assumption* by Titian and next to it Sansovino's tomb of Galesio Nichesola.

The north door of the *duomo* leads into a courtyard and a passage to the cloister. On the left are sections of mosaic pavement that probably date from the sixth century. The cloister itself is a simple romanesque composition, with arcades on three sides resting on double columns of marble. The gallery to the right is two-tiered, and also preserves more of the mosaic pavement. As you return up the passageway you'll be facing the porch of the twelfth-century church of Santa Elena; on the left of the porch are arcades from the Carolingian period. Return to the *duomo*, turn left,

and go through the last door along the aisle, which leads to an excavated section of the former, eighth-century cathedral. If Santa Elena is closed, glass doors here allow you to glimpse the interior. To the right is a doorway beneath an empty niche. This leads to another twelfth-century church, San Giovanni in Fonte, built in simple basilica style. On the walls you'll see a few medieval and even byzantine frescoes, but the masterpiece here is the astonishing romanesque font of 1220. It is carved from a single block of marble, yet it is the size of a large jacuzzi. Each of its six sides is carved with reliefs of scenes from the life of Christ.

On leaving the *duomo* by the west door, you'll see on your right the cathedral library, one of the oldest in Europe, containing manuscripts dating back to AD 710. Continue down Stradone Pacifico, then bear left down Via Sole, and left again down Via San Egidio. Turn left into Via San Mammaso and on the left you'll see one of the best *palazzi* in an area crammed with them: Palazzo Miniscalchi, indifferently frescoed but with beautifully carved spandrels and capitals, especially on the first floor windows. Continue down Via San Egidio. At the end of the street on the left is another Venetian-gothic *palazzo*, the pock-marked Palazzo Franchini, which has an attractive courtyard. At the corner, turn right down Via Emilei to the stark brick church of Sant'Eufemia, consecrated in 1331. It retains its elegant gothic west door of coloured marble, but the windows have been classicized. Beneath the windows are two contrasted tombs: the heavy pink marble sarcophagus of Cavalcan Cavalcani (1279), and Sammicheli's coldly elegant neo-classical tomb of Tomaso Lavagnoli (1550).

The interior, with its great breadth and length, would make a fine railway station. The south transept and the south wall of the choir retain damaged frescoes by the fourteenth-century artist Martino da Verona. The south absidal chapel, Cappella Spolverini, still has its gothic appearance and its full set of frescoes, some of which are early fifteenth-century, while others, plus a triptych altar-piece, are by Caroto. At the far end of the choir is the fifteenth-century Dal Verme monument, adorned with statues. The sixth chapel along the south aisle contains a medieval bas-relief of the Madonna and Child. Connoisseurs of religious gore should not miss the medieval *Pietà* halfway down the north aisle. It seems to have come straight from the props cupboard at Hammer films.

On leaving the church, turn left down Via Adua. Turn right, and you'll come to the Roman arch called Porta dei Borsari. Pass through, for the other side is far more richly ornamented, all in white stone. Continue into Corso Cavour, once the main street of Roman Verona and now grandly packed with *palazzi* of various periods: no. 10, the Venetian-gothic Casa Pozzoni; no. 11, Palazzo Scannagatti, an especially lavish renaissance palace; and no. 19, Sammicheli's richly carved Palazzo Bevilacqua. To the left is the partially romanesque church of Santi Apostoli, which has a number of tombs attached limpet-like to its outer walls. A north chapel contains a fine medieval painted Crucifix. Some fragmentary twelfth-century frescoes are preserved in the hall that leads to the sacristy. Steps from the sacristy lead down to a domed chapel, originally a fifth-century martyrium, then a church dedicated in 751 to Saints Tosca and Tueteria; it was rebuilt in 1160 in the shape of a Greek cross. Its contents include a romanesque font, an altar with a fifteenth-century sculpted group of the Madonna and saints, and two fine medieval tombs. Next to these buildings is a courtyard with a pretty two-storeyed loggia on double columns of pink marble.

On the other side of Corso Cavour is the well-restored church of San Lorenzo, better observed from the river bank, where its gentle romanesque design is more apparent. The church is remarkable in possessing not only a campanile but two round towers attached to the west façade. The lofty interior is one of the loveliest in Verona: double arcades, and tall open galleries above them. Apart from fragmentary frescoes in the south chapel and renaissance tombs along the north aisle, the church is refreshingly free of significant later embellishments, in part because it was damaged during World War II.

From Corso Cavour one can easily make out the bulk of Castelvecchio, a huge brick pile of seven towers enclosed within battlemented walls and surrounded by a dry moat and the river. It was built under Cangrande II in the 1350s and the architect was Francesco Bevilacqua, whose tomb is in the martyrium at Santi Apostoli. In subsequent centuries the castle was used mostly as a barracks, and only in 1925 did it become the museum that it remains today. Just before you reach the castle, you will see on your right the Arco dei Gavi, a first-century AD Roman arch. A city gate during the early Middle Ages, it was destroyed by French troops in 1805, and reconstructed from fragments as recently as 1933. Understandably it is somewhat the worse for wear, but still provides an interesting contrast of Roman grandeur side by side with Scaligeri might.

Before entering the castle courtyard, walk on a few metres to the south wing, from where you can follow a path through the castle and on to the Ponte Scaligero, or Ponte Merlato, with the immense keep of 1375 leaning, as it were, on your right shoulder. The bridge, also built during the reign of Cangrande II, is visible from many points along this stretch of the Adige, and it is a magnificent sight, with its defensive V-shaped projections between each span. Like the other bridges of Verona, it was destroyed during the war but has been meticulously rebuilt.

The castle interior has been thoroughly gutted. The sequence of rooms begins with early medieval work, including an elaborate sarcophagus of 1179 and a collection of fifth-century Lombard burial ornaments. The following three rooms contain medieval reliefs, tabernacles, and statuary, and a harrowing fourteenth-century *Crucifixion*. Most of these items came from churches that have been destroyed. After leaving this wing, you will cross a bridge into the main part of the keep. Among the exhibits are a fine collection of frescoes, including an expressive thirteenth-century *Crucifixion*, a weighty fourteenth-century *Madonna Enthroned*, fascinating preliminary drafts from Altichiero's workshop, and a fine fourteenth-century

The exquisite romanesque arcades of the church of San Lorenzo.

Above A Roman gate, the Arco dei Gavi, now enjoying splendid isolation in Verona.

Right Verona's finest bridge links the Scaliger castle with the opposite bank of the River Adige.

Crucifixion attributed to Turone. The many medieval paintings include polyptychs by Turone (1360) and School of Altichiero, the enchanting *Madonna del Rosetto* by Stefano da Zevio, and a moving *Madonna della Quaglia* attributed, plausibly, to Pisanello. The main room contains two fine painted Crucifixes, and a characterful *St Catherine of Siena* by Spanzotti. These rooms are also well stocked with works of indifferent quality by Jacopo Bellini (1400–70/1).

On the floor above, the main gallery is awash with mediocrity, but the side rooms are full of good things: a charming *Madonna* by Carlo Crivelli (c.1430–c.1495), full, as usual, of sideshows, a melodious *Sacra conversazione* by Francesco Francia (c.1450–1517), a watchful *Madonna* by Francesco Bonsignori (c.1455–1519), a surprise given the ineptitude of most of his output, characterful paintings by Bartolommeo Montagna, a serene *Crucifixion* by Gentile Bellini (1429/30–1507), and two even more serene Madonnas by Giovanni Bellini. In the next section you come to the weaponry collections, and gain access to the riverside battlements.

The bridge leading to the remaining galleries contains the striking equestrian statue of Cangrande I. Most of the remaining galleries are devoted to sixteenth-century work, much of it conventionalized and routine. The contrast helps one comprehend the vaguely Ruskinian notion of the purity of feeling in medieval art – even if half the painters couldn't draw. But there's much to admire here too: a hilarious Caroto portrait of a boy who can't draw either, a Francesco Morone fresco of the Madonna and saints, Girolamo dai Libri's verdant *Madonna dell'Ombretto*, some doubtful Tintorettos (except for the fine *Adoration of the Shepherds*), a *Deposition* by Veronese, some lively canvases by Paolo Farinati (c.1524–c.1606), a portrait of an old man by Marcantonio Bassetti (1588–1630), and, in the last room, G. D. Tiepolo's *Four Saints*. From Castelvecchio, Via Roma leads back to Piazza Brà and the ever welcome cafés of the Liston.

The districts of the city outside the central loop have a lesser concentration of major monuments, but should on no account be slighted, for they are full of interest.

From the Arena, walk behind the Palazzo Municipale till you come, on your left, to Stradone Maffei, which turns into Stradone San Fermo. You will pass *palazzi* along both sides of the street, and the closed church of San Pietro Incarnario on the right. The street brings you to the west façade of San Fermo Maggiore. The exterior of this fascinating church is a jumble, since, like the basilica of St Francis in Assisi, it was originally built as a double-decker church. The upper church was rebuilt by the Minorites during the gothic period, yet elements of the romanesque structure, notably the campanile and the west façade, remain. There is also a confusion of building materials, with brick and tufa used seemingly at random. Walk to the east end, and you will see a much gabled and pinnacled roofline, and the campanile soaring into the sky. Returning to the west end, you will pass the magnificent north porch with its immense fifteenth-century baldacchino sheltering a broad flight of pink marble steps that leads to the portal of 1363. The west end is more evidently romanesque. To the left of the door is the canopied tomb (1385) of the Scaligeri's family doctor, Avertino Fracastoro, with a contemporary inscription beneath. South of the church you can see the cloisters, partly frescoed, which were rebuilt after bomb damage during World War II.

Enter the upper church from the north door. The aisleless interior is lavishly frescoed and has a truly spectacular coffered ship's keel roof of 1314, like an upturned galleon. It would be tedious to describe all the frescoes. The majority are fourteenth-century, and many are of excellent quality. At the west end of the north aisle is the fifteenth-century Brenzoni tomb by Nanni di Bartolo; cherubs draw back the curtains to reveal the resurrected Christ while soldiers collapse in a heap beneath the tomb. Above the tomb is an infinitely delicate fresco of the Annunciation (1426) by the great Pisanello, who outshines all his contemporaries, even, as here, in his first extant work. As in the Santa Anastasia frescoes, fragility and delicacy of feeling combine with an unerring firmness of line.

Opposite the monument are frescoes that depict the awful fate that befell four Franciscan missionaries in

India. Walk down the south aisle and you will soon see the marble pulpit of 1396 with its elaborately carved canopy and its very fine frescoes by Martino da Verona. Just beyond the pulpit a chapel contains the elaborate but chunky early fifteenth-century tomb of Barnaba da Morano. This, like the pulpit, is the work of Antonio da Mestre. Next to this chapel is an altar, beneath which is an *Entombment* of 1523. In the south absidal chapel is another *Entombment* from the previous century. Cross to the north aisle where you will find tucked away a very plain chapel that simply contains two superb renaissance tombs, the monuments to Girolamo and Marcantonio Torriani, whose death masks gaze out from the very top. The tombs date from the early sixteenth century and are the work either of Andrea Briosco or Andrea Crispo da Padova.

From the south transept you descend to the lower church, where the date 1065 appears on one of the columns. The church has a nave and two aisles, but the nave is supported by a further row of piers of irregular shape, many of them frescoed. Unfortunately floods, notably those of 1757, severely damaged the lower church, which remained closed until its restoration twenty years ago. What remains is very precious, since some of the frescoes are clearly romanesque, a rarity even in Verona. In the broad apse is a superb fourteenth-century wooden Crucifix.

On leaving the church turn right and you will soon see a bridge, the Ponte Navi. Turn left down Via Leoni, pass the excavations in the middle of the street, and on your right you will see Porta Leoni on the corner. Only one bay survives of a much larger Roman gateway through which the principal thoroughfare of the city, the Cardo, passed. The original gate was brick, but the Romans added an elaborate and unusually elegant façade of white Valpolicella stone. Although worn by time, the carving of the cornices and capitals must have been of high quality.

Return to the Ponte Navi and cross it. This bank of the Adige is less imposing than the city centre, a district of workshops, neighbourhood groceries and bars, and unpretentious restaurants. You will find few tourists in its streets. On the right, as you are crossing the bridge, you can see the rusticated façade of Sammicheli's Palazzo Pompei (1531), now the natural sciences museum. Once you are on terra firma walk straight up Via San Paolo, past the church of that name. Of romanesque origin, the church has often been reconstructed, most recently after World War II. In the south transept there is an expressive *Madonna and Saints* by Veronese; in the choir a more stylized treatment of the same subject by Gian Francesco Caroto, enlivened by rather too virtuoso a demonstration of perspective; and in a south chapel yet another version by Caroto's better known contemporary, Girolamo dai Libri.

After 200 m turn left on to Vicolo Terra. You will emerge near the forecourt of the fifteenth-century church of Santi Nazaro e Celso, although it actually contains not their relics but those óf San Biagio. The church has a plain brick gothic façade, with a round window over the portal, a formulation one finds in many Verona churches. The interior is mostly neo-classical, but the north transept chapel preserves fading but impressive frescoes, mostly by Bartolommeo Montagna, depicting assorted saints enclosed within complex painted architectural motifs. Over the high altar is a fine painted Crucifix, and in the south transept is a polychrome sculpture of a seated Madonna and Child – if you can see it through the gloom. The sanctuary contains inlaid cupboards of high quality, if lacking the imaginative flair of those at the nearby church of Santa Maria in Organo. The organ doors have painted doors by Battista Brusasorci depicting musicians on a balcony.

At this church I perfected a vital art: inspecting a church while a wedding is in progress. I lurked for what seemed like hours, but made my move down the aisle as a Neapolitan-style tenor up in the organ loft wrenched every drip of emotion from Gounod's 'Ave Maria'. Even the singer seemed embarrassed by his performance when it was all over. I hid happily near the saint's bones until the throng waded out of the church to waylay the newly-weds with rice and tooting horns.

From the church walk down Via Muro Padri to the

eighteenth-century Giardini Giusti, an elegant flowing design of terraces and paths, and one of Verona's loveliest and most precious amenities, hidden on the terraces behind the *palazzo* of the same name, which was built before the gardens, in 1580. The English traveller Thomas Coryate was clearly seduced by the gardens' loveliness as long ago as 1611, when he described them as 'a second paradise, a passing delectable place of solace.' Half a century later John Evelyn considered them to be the finest in all of Europe. By 1786, when Goethe visited them, the cypresses were already immense. The damage done by the force of nature in the form of lightning and by the hand of man in the form of war damage has taken its toll, as have the clumsy alterations made in the last century to the gardens' layout. Nonetheless the Giardini Giusti remain a haven from which to escape the bustle of downtown Verona by strolling along the cypress-bordered walks and lawns, or resting at the charming renaissance loggia with its slender arcades at the top of the hill, from where one can enjoy the splendid views of the town.

On leaving the gardens, continue down this street until you reach Santa Maria in Organo. The façade is a fairly grim exercise by Sammicheli, although to the left of the forecourt is a plain but pretty cloister. The interior is surprisingly lofty. Rounded arcades rest on piers with massive capitals, all carved differently. The painted barrel vaults simulate a coffered ceiling. The church was founded in the seventh century, and some of the original materials were reused in the crypt. The next building campaigns took place in the twelfth and fifteenth centuries. The campanile dates from 1520. The whole church is frescoed but many are damaged, and the overall quality is not very high. In the north absidal chapel is a curiosity: a thirteenth-century wooden statue of Christ on an ass.

The steep hillside setting as well as the architectural remains make the Roman theatre one of Verona's finest if least visited attractions.

The glory of the church is its woodwork. In the choir are forty-one exquisitely carved and inlaid stalls and a lectern (1491–9), all by Giovanni da Verona. The workmanship is exquisite, with depictions of street scenes, bowls of cherries and musical instruments, as well as religious emblems. From one side of the lectern a hamster is shown peeking out, and from the other an owl. The stalls in the sacristy, also by Giovanni da Verona (1457–1525), are, if anything, even more refined, and certainly more complex in design, than those in the choir. Note, among other felicities, how brilliantly he has carved, in a space a mere nine inches high, piles of martial emblems and other bric-à-brac at the base of the columns. The sacristy cupboards are inlaid with more painted panels, possibly by Domenico Brusasorci (1516–67). There are also some lively medieval stone panels depicting the Madonna and Saints, and the Crucifixion. The sacristy also has the most vivid frescoes, by Domenico and Francesco Morone, portraying Benedictine monks and nuns in white robes dramatically outlined against a black background. The crypt of the church, accessible from near the sacristy, has a fourteenth-century altar-piece by Giovanni di Rigino.

From Santa Maria return to what began as Via Muro Padri and is now Via Santa Maria, and continue to the gothic church of Santa Chiara, which seems permanently closed. Just before you reach it a lane to the right leads to San Giovanni in Valle. A twelfth-century church, it is uncharacteristic of Veronese architecture in that it is built from yellow stone (except for the much later belfry). One range of the romanesque cloister, with double marble columns, survives south of the church. A few steps lead down into the nave, but most of the nave and the choir are in fact raised on a balustraded platform over the crypt, which contains some early Christian marble sarcophagi and pre-romanesque columns. There are few furnishings of interest, as the church was severely damaged by bombs in 1944. Yet it is worth visiting, both because it is a lucid dignified church and because it is enjoyable to stroll through this relatively tranquil and hilly corner of the city.

Descend to the river and keep walking north, and you will soon reach the Roman theatre, set against the hillside beneath a grove of cypresses. Compared to the Arena, it is modest in size, but the setting is attractive and it is used for Shakespearian performances during the summer months. To the right, reached by a double staircase, is the church of Santi Siro e Libera, with its frescoed portal. To the left there is a kind of *ad hoc* lapidary museum; from here steps lead up not only to the upper tiers of the theatre, but higher still to various terraces from which there are fine views of the old city. From here a lift conveys visitors to the archaeological museum, housed in a former monastery. This contains mosaics, amphorae, busts, figurines, glassware, and some damaged statues. A pretty cloister shelters some more mosaics and inscriptions, and in an adjoining chapel there is, incongruously, a fine medieval triptych. More exhibits are reached down the steps from the cloister. Labelling is erratic, and the museum is rather a feeble effort.

Behind the museum, screened by cypresses at the top of the hill, is the Castel San Pietro, reached by steps from near the Ponte Pietra. The castle that once stood here was largely destroyed by the French, and the site was transformed by the Austrians into their barracks in 1854. Follow the river bank north. On the right you will pass Ponte Pietra, a Roman and medieval bridge destroyed, like all Verona's bridges, during World War II, but painstakingly reconstructed and now open only to pedestrians. Just beyond the bridge is the church of San Stefano. Originally a cathedral, the extant church is essentially twelfth-century, with a bold octagonal campanile. It has an austere façade of alternating bands of stone and brick. The south aisle chapel, dedicated to the Veronese martyrs buried in the church, is a lively baroque design, and contains three appropriately gory but not contemptible altar paintings. In the south aisle there is a crude but powerful fresco of the Crucifixion, close to the steps that descend to the crypt. The choir and transepts are raised on a platform above the crypt. As you mount the choir steps you will see on the right a massive romanesque statue of St Peter seated. Behind the altar there is evidence of the preceding structures (as there is on the exterior, just behind the tower), and a few steep steps give access to an ambulatory with columns that belonged to the pre-romanesque church. Much of the interior is frescoed; some in the ambulatory date from 1200 but are fragmentary, and the only ones of any interest are to the left of the altar: an *Annunciation* by either Stefano da Zevio or Martino da Verona, and a *Coronation of the Virgin* attributed to Altichiero.

Continue along the river. On the other bank you can see the tower of the bishops' palace, as well as the *duomo* campanile. You soon come to the church of San Giorgio in Braida. The brutal massiveness of Sammicheli's unfinished campanile is reminiscent of his façade at Santa Maria in Organo. The modelling of the interior and the dome are also by Sammicheli. The imposing façade gives access to a broad and aisleless interior. Over the west door is a Tintoretto, it is claimed, but the painting is so darkened it could be by anyone. Among the better paintings are Gian Francesco Caroto's *Annunciation* on either side of the choir arch, Girolamo dai Libri's *Virgin Enthroned*, and Veronese's swirling *Martyrdom of St George* in the choir itself, which also has furnishings of high quality: Sammicheli's gently curving neo-classical altar, richly carved stalls, and six bronze statuettes over the balustrade separating choir and nave (and two more such statuettes by Angelo Rossi over the fonts). Over the south aisle is a splendid carved choir gallery supported on brackets which themselves rest on Ionic columns and winged griffins.

Just beyond San Giorgio is Sammicheli's Porta San Giorgio, faced with white stone and dated 1525. Walk through the little park to the Ponte Garibaldi, and stay on this side of the Adige until you reach the Ponte Scaligero, which you should cross. Turn right when you come to the Corso, and you will soon reach the tiny thirteenth-century church of San Zeno in Oratorio.

The imposing church of San Giorgio in Braida is one of many major buildings in Verona designed by Sammicheli.

Enter, along Vicolo San Zeno, through a gateway on which two eighteenth-century statues of saints mount guard. San Zeno is a very simple and often restored church of three arcades. Over the west door an early medieval fresco depicts the Crucifixion; in the north aisle is a small fourteenth-century carved tabernacle; and at the back of the choir sits an ancient wooden statue of San Zeno.

This attractive church is not to be confused with the masterpiece called San Zeno Maggiore. This is reached by following the river for a few hundred metres, then cutting left. A large piazza faces the church, which was begun in 1120 and completed a century later, except for the apse, which dates from the late fourteenth century. Zeno was appointed bishop of Verona in 362 and died in 380. As many as five churches probably stood here before the present one was erected. It seems strange that such veneration, and architectural splendour, have been lavished on so obscure a figure. Apart from the fact that he was born in Africa – not that unusual in fourth-century Christendom – virtually nothing is known about him. His biography was written by a Veronese called Coronatus in the eighth century, but scholars insist that its factual content is negligible. I doubt that there are many contemporary readers of his sermons, which are still in print, but we can be grateful that this mysterious figure inspired the marvellous artistic response that we see before us.

The immense church does not stand alone. Three other buildings stand alongside it, and since this is a less crowded part of Verona, each of them is boldly delineated against the sky. To the left is a tall brick castellated tower, a fourteenth-century remnant of an abbey that once stood here. Then there is the crisp symmetrical west front of the church, blind arcades rising up the flanks of its Lombard façade. Horizontal lines of brick and tufa carry the eye to the rear of the church, uninterrupted by transepts. There at the back, close to the church, is the tall, slender, elegant campanile (begun in 1045 and completed by Maestro Martino in 1173), marked by the same horizontal bands, and capped with two bell stages beneath a conical turret. Further to the right is the ancient but disused church of San Procolo.

The façade of San Zeno is splendid. Beneath the large rose window of about 1200 by Maestro Brioloto – the first of its kind in Italy – is the portal by Maestro Nicolò, who also designed the *duomo* portal. Its columns rest on the backs of two stone lions, and it is richly ornamented with eight large reliefs on either side of the door, a polychrome tympanum in low relief, and further carvings on the canopy, including crouched figures represented as holding up its weight. The relief panels include familiar biblical scenes such as the creation of Eve and the Flight into Egypt, as well as allegorical scenes. And in the centre of it all are the great bronze doors, so varied in subject matter – Old and New Testaments, as well as the life of San Zeno – and, though often crude in execution to a modern eye, immensely vivid as each scene is individually styled and realized. The oldest panels date from about 1100, the later ones from about a century later.

A passage to the left of the church leads into the lovely cloister of 1123, with its twinned columns. Although some of the arcades are rounded and others pointed, there is remarkable unity of style here. The cloister walls are lined with medieval tombs, some of which contain Scaligeri bones. The east range gives access to St Benedict's chapel, supported on a hotch-potch of piers of different shapes and sizes – one way to use up old stones. After you enter the church itself, mount the steps at the west end to enjoy the full majesty of the interior: its breadth, the mighty arches spanning the nave, the purity of line and yet complexity of articulation (with capitals copiously carved), the seemingly endless horizontal projection of the wooden roof of 1386, and then the sudden descent into the half-visible crypt, with the platform of the choir above, its balustrade lined with elegantly carved mid thirteenth-century statues of Christ and the Apostles. Only the distant apse, rebuilt in the fourteenth century and rib-vaulted, mars the unity, though not the beauty.

The nave of San Zeno Maggiore, Verona, one of the most majestic romanesque interiors of the Veneto.

199

The furnishings are sparse but of high quality. On the west wall is an immense painted Crucifix; in front of it a large arcaded romanesque font of 1194. The north aisle is terminated by a great broad shallow porphyry dish from Roman times. The medieval frescoes along the south aisle wall, although damaged, are remarkably lucid, and generally of better quality than those opposite. Half-way down the south aisle is a bizarre altar, probably thirteenth-century, supported on ugly knotted columns that rest on the backs of a lion and bull; there's also an isolated twisted column on the north side of the steps leading down to the crypt. Beyond the altar are some contemporaneous frescoes, notably of Saints Catherine and Lucy. On the south wall of the raised section are slightly later frescoes, some scrawled over with centuries-old graffiti. Over the raised section, a fine fresco above the arcades depicting the Madonna with saints and kneeling monks is by the School of Altichiero, as is the *Crucifixion* on the north wall. A beautiful sarcophagus with panelled reliefs, primitive but powerful, doubles as the altar, while the lectern consists of two recycled late eleventh-century statues in niches. The high altar has a painting worthy of this great church: a triptych by Mantegna (1459), the *Madonna with Angels and Eight Saints*; the predella panels are copies of the originals Napoleon stole for the Louvre. In the north absidal chapel is a large painted statue of Zeno, shown smiling, probably at the fish suspended from his crook. To the left, on the north wall, is a rich selection of medieval frescoes. The artists weren't afraid of repetition. There are at least three huge St Christophers and at least five Crucifixions on the walls of the church. The lovely *Annunciation* on the choir arch is late fourteenth-century and attributed to Martino da Verona.

The crypt is of eleventh-century origin although the carved capitals date mostly from the early thirteenth century. The structure rests on forty-eight capitals,

No two panels are alike in the twelfth-century bronze doors of San Zeno Maggiore in Verona.

giving nine aisles. The altars are mostly reliquaries of local saints, including Zeno, who rests in the gothic apse. Note how the massive compound piers that support the church roof rise from the floor of the crypt, entirely blocking some of the aisles.

From San Zeno head south for a few hundred metres till you see the slender campanile of San Bernardino, which is approached through a large, somewhat tatty cloister. This Franciscan church, begun in the 1450s, is a plain gothic brick structure, lightly embellished with turrets. The interior is lopsided, with a very broad nave but only one aisle. The first chapel is filled with frescoes by Nicola Giolfino portraying the life of St Francis, completed in 1522. The east chapel, the Cappella Avanzi, is panelled with paintings, mostly flat and conventional, by an anthology of sixteenth-century Veronese painters – Caroto, Francesco Morone, Giolfino – but they are highly coloured and the overall effect, aided by the gilt framing, is impressive. A fine polychrome *Deposition*, realistically carved, presents a mournful scene behind a grille. Tucked next to the choir is the domed Cappella Pellegrini (1527) by Sammicheli, luminous and with finely carved pilasters and a coffered ceiling, but cold-hearted. The design is modelled on the Roman mausoleums that Sammicheli would have studied earlier in his career when he was living in Rome. The organ, which has painted doors by Domenico Morone, rests on a prettily decorated and carved bracket dated 1481. The triptych by Benaglia of 1462 in the choir bears a by no means coincidental resemblance to Mantegna's altar-piece at San Zeno. Next to the church entrance is the door into the monastery, which has an attractive two-storey cloister. The former library painted by Domenico Morone from 1494 to 1503 is open to visitors.

From here it is a short walk south to the great mass of the five-bay Porta Palio, the last work of Sammicheli, completed in 1557. Behind the façade, there is an immense arched passage, followed by the brick walls that hem in the vaulted interior bays. The façade seen when approaching the city is far stronger, its three bays separated by pairs of Doric half-pillars, and above, a massive cornice. From here you can walk along the edge of the city, passing the zoo, and return to Porta Nuova.

The region to the south of the city is hardly one of outstanding natural beauty, but it is nonetheless of considerable interest for its surviving medieval fortifications, a reminder of the constant insecurities of life under the warlords. Begin by heading west of Verona to Sona and Sommacampagna. Avoid threading your way through the wasteland south of Verona, which is encumbered with roadworks, tangled *autostrade*, industrial estates, customs sheds and airports, and take the *autostrada* (Milano direction) to Sommacampagna and head north to Sona. From its shapely town square a road leads north-west, passing rambling nineteenth-century villas, to the four-square church of Santi Quirico e Giulitta, which is adorned with barely competent but pretty frescoes in pastel shades. At Sommacampagna the villas are enclosed behind high walls close to the top of the village. In the cemetery is a charming romanesque chapel with contemporary frescoes, though I have never found it open.

Drive south to Villafranca, on the southern edge of the Veneto. Originally intended by Verona to keep the Mantuans at bay, Villafranca had a bloody time of it in the fifteenth century, and was finally captured by the Dukes of Ferrara in 1487. Although partly ruined, the castle here, grandly situated at the end of the broad Corso Vittorio Emanuele, is still immensely imposing, a compact complex of towers and bays, with a huge brick central tower and a battlemented gateway. On either side of the castle and behind it are high castellated walls of stone and bands of brick. Just to the left of the castle is the entrance to the Museum of the Risorgimento, located here as Villafranca played a major role in the reunification of Italy. You can skirt the castle walls through a shady park that encircles them. The castle has been undergoing restoration for some time, and when the works, invariably protracted in Italy, are completed, it should be reopened to visitors.

If you walk down the Corso one block and turn left, you will soon come to Villafranca's other claim to fame:

the unremarkable house where in July 1859 Napoleon III and Emperor Franz Josef of Austria signed an armistice agreement. A few kilometres to the south, just beyond Grezzano, is the vast Villa Canossa, designed by Sammicheli but since modified. More a palace than a villa, Canossa is surrounded by an equally immense complex of farm buildings. Despite its grandeur, the villa's unvarying bays are somewhat monotonous. The handsome and well maintained little neo-classical church behind, with its elegantly carved fluted pilasters and cornice, is well worth a glance.

Return to Villafranca and drive west towards Valeggio sul Mincio. You'll pass close to the village of Custoza, which gives its name to an underrated white wine made from grapes grown on these gentle slopes. In the fourteenth century fortifications stretched all the way from Villafranca to Vallegio, and a few scraps are still visible along the road. Vallegio's Scaliger castle can be seen most dramatically from this road, its four lofty and asymmetrical towers rising into the sky. Even more dramatic are the remains of the extraordinary late fourteenth-century Ponte Visconteo, an immense fortified bridge crossing the River Mincio. It is half-ruined yet still serviceable, and the road passes beneath two immense broad towers. Just to the left of the bridge is the hamlet of Borghetto, also fortified. From its weir there is a good view of the bridge and the river. This is a charming spot, and the restaurants at Borghetto make the most of it. At time of writing the castle was being restored and was inaccessible.

Drive north to Peschiera del Garda at the foot of the lake of that name. This has long been a garrison town, and the Venetian fortifications and gates and their Austrian amplifications have been well preserved. Curiously, the town within the star-shaped walls is spacious and attractive, but Peschiera and its surroundings at the foot of Lake Garda have become so commercialized that its hard to imagine anyone, other

At Vallegio a magnificent medieval bridge crosses the River Mincio beneath the imposing Scaliger fortress.

than a twelve-year-old on a loose leash, deriving much pleasure from the place. Just south of the town is the sixteenth-century sanctuary of Madonna del Frassino. The baroque interior has integrity and consistency of design, and the elaborate gilt organ behind the altar adds a more playful touch. Adjoining the church is a Franciscan monastery, with its complex of cloisters and cemeteries.

Drive north up the lakeshore to Lazise. From the moment one glimpses the lake it is easy to discern why its shores are so popular with northern visitors. (The citizens assume that all visitors to the town are German-speaking, and they are usually right.) The upper parts of the shore are dramatically situated at the foot of mountains and cliffs, while here, at the southern end, the landscape is more gentle and consoling. The climate is mildness itself, invariably welcome, even in winter, after the rigours of the weather to the north of the Alps. Lazise is a pretty little town, though very touristy, set snugly within partially surviving medieval walls and gates. The harbour is built into the town, off the lakefront, and on one side of it are the surviving fourteenth-century customs shed and the much-altered romanesque church, which contains fragmentary medieval frescoes of mediocre quality. On the south side of town are more substantial remains of the old walls, as well as the Scaliger castle.

Continue north to Cisano. Just before the village is an olive-oil museum. Cisano is more tranquil than Lazise, with a charming marina and lakeside promenade. The church has a low romanesque campanile and some decidedly primitive goings-on along the west front, in the form of carvings and capitals that could well be from the eighth century.

A few kilometres further north is Bardolino, with the same charms and the same drawbacks as the other little towns along the lake. Away from the water, up a lane, is the minute but very tall eighth-century church of San Zeno, with its well-preserved capitals. Along the

The hamlet of Borghetto clings to the banks of the River Mincio near Vallegio.

main road is the pretty twelfth-century church of San Severo, with its charming zigzag pattern on the apse. The interior is equally delightful, with faded frescoes in the north aisle and above the arcades. There is a remarkable sunken apse, a kind of open crypt. Within the old town are a few *palazzi* as well as the large lakeshore villa and winery of Countess Guerrieri-Rizzardi, a leading producer of the light refreshing red wine named after the village, although the zone of production extends back into the hills. At Bardolino, indeed, the essentially flat shoreline begins to sprout some sizable hills, and as one continues up the lake the scenery becomes increasingly dramatic.

Soon you will reach Garda itself, a small, even cosy little town, embraced and protected by the hills. Although very ancient, little remains of its distant past. In a square by the lakefront stands the fifteenth-century Palazzo del Capitano, with its delicate gothic windows of pink marble. At the northern edge of the old town is the early renaissance Palazzo Fregoso, and at the southern end the church, where a barely visible Palma Giovane hangs above the west door. A door in the south aisle gives access to a plain two-storey cloister. High above the town, but most easily reached from Bardolino, is the Eremo, a seventeenth-century Camaldolensian monastery. Male visitors may enter the monastery for services only; women are excluded at all times, but may console themselves with the fine view of the lake.

West of Garda a headland known as Punta San Vigilio pokes out into the lake. At its tip is the very simple Villa Guarienti, attributed to Sammicheli. Cobbled lanes and modest stone buildings, all impeccably restored, surround the villa, and one of the outbuildings shelters a lemon grove. Down by the tiny harbour is another villa, now a hotel, and a café with tables delightfully positioned out on the jetty.

A few kilometres north is the little town of Torri del Benaco. The Scaligeri castle, secure behind high crenellated walls, houses a small museum that documents local occupations, such as fishing and olive cultivation, and includes a small botanic garden. Some delightful old houses decorate the port and some of the

back streets of the village. A promenade connects the port with the tenth-century tower supposed to have been built by Berengar (*c*.900–966), king of what then constituted Italy, and named after him. The church next to the tower contains a pretty eighteenth-century organ and gallery.

Continuing up the lakeside you will see, just before Castelletto di Brenzone, the cemetery, and alongside it a rough-hewn romanesque church dedicated to the ubiquitous San Zeno. Just north of Brenzone itself is the lakeside hamlet of Assenza, where the tiny church has mediocre but nonetheless interesting fragmentary frescoes in a byzantine style. The road leads to Malcesine, at the foot of the wooded slopes of Monte Baldo, and from here a cable car transports visitors 1800 m up the mountain. Malcesine is a bustling but pleasant resort, with an extensive old quarter around the castle. From the dock and from the restaurants built out into the water are lovely views on to the wilder west shore of Lake Garda with its clifftop villages. To the south a promontory is contoured with cypress trees. Narrow cobbled lanes lead to the dramatically situated thirteenth-century castle, with its frescoes and museum and modern art gallery. Between the castle and the delightful little port is the town hall, the Palazzo dei Capitani del Lago, with its early-renaissance fenestration. In 1786 Goethe stayed in what is now the Hotel San Marco down by the port. Like so many of these lake resorts, Malcesine has become a *de facto* German colony.

Return southwards by the inland route, past the hill resort of San Zeno and down to Affi, a few kilometres inland from Bardolino. Affi is split in two, one village on the hillside, the other on the plain. In the lower is the broad, mustard-coloured seventeenth-century Villa Poggi, flanked by arcaded agricultural wings and set in pleasant grounds. From Affi, drive east across the *autostrada* and the River Adige. Take the Trento road for a few kilometres till you reach Volargne, where the

There is no more lovely spot along the shores of Lake Garda than the promontory of San Vigilio.

Villa del Bene, partly built by Sammicheli, is located. A fine portal leads into a courtyard, and the open loggia of the villa is frescoed, as are most of the rooms. These frescoes are well preserved, and here and there one can glimpse earlier designs exposed beneath the plaster. A side wing leads to the chapel and tower. The villa is empty but well cared for by the most welcoming of custodians.

Return down the main road to the turning for Sant'Ambrogio. Perched high above this village, its tall romanesque campanile visible from afar, is San Giorgio, with its very beautiful eleventh-century church. The interior is long and dark, with only tiny lancets in the clerestory and apse providing any light. A very rare feature of the church is the eighth-century ciborium, reconstructed but authentic, over the altar. The capitals and all four sides are ornamented. The frescoes in the apsidal west end are twelfth-century, and the most important is a stern and authoritative *Christ in Majesty*, painted with a skilful use of the curved space. Close by stands the massive romanesque font, decorated with blind arcading. From the south apse a door leads into a pretty little cloister, its brightness welcome after the austerity of the church. Stroll across to the terrace opposite the church, from which there is a panoramic view of Lake Garda.

East of Sant'Ambrogio is Gargagnago, one of the villages of the Valpolicella wine region. Within a walled park is the villa originally built by Dante's son in the fourteenth century and still inhabited by his descendant Pieralvise Serego Alighieri, whose estate produces some of the best Recioto in the region.

Towards Verona lie the villages of San Pietro in Cariano, with its attractive little municipal square, and San Floriano, whose church has a good romanesque campanile, though its patchwork construction of tufa, brick, and white stone takes getting used to. A charming renaissance loggia with a fresco of the Crucifixion adjoins the church. Return towards

The lakeside town of Torri del Benaco faces the wilder eastern shore of Lake Garda.

A richly carved baroque doorway enlivens a plain façade at Malcesine.

Even a modest parish church such as that at San Floriano is enriched with carving and ornament.

Sant'Ambrogio but bear north to Fumane. From here take the Mazzurega road, and you will soon see the battlemented tower that gives the mid sixteenth-century Villa della Torre its name. Next to the tower is Sammicheli's octagonal chapel; he may have built the villa too. Unfortunately the house is hard to see, as it faces into a courtyard, reminiscent of the Villa del Bene at Volargne. The roof has distinctive turret-like chimneys.

Above **Spring blossoms enhance the pastoral beauty of the remote valleys around Santa Anna d'Alfaedo.**

Right **In the grounds of Villa Santa Sofia at Pedemonte, one of Palladio's most astonishing villas.**

Fumane is one of the best-preserved wine villages in the heart of the Valpolicella Classico zone, but these lovely valleys, once filled with vines, are gradually being built up. Take the road north towards Marano and Santa Anna d'Alfaedo, passing the cement works that now defaces this once charming valley. On the left are the quarries from which the marble known as Rosso di Verona is extracted. Just before Santa Anna turn right, following signs for Ponte di Veia. This huge stone bridge, elegantly shaped yet formed naturally across the valley, is one of the largest of its kind in the world. Inside the caves at either end signs of prehistoric habitation have been found.

Return past the village of Fane through lovely scenery towards another wine village, Negrar, recognizable by its immense romanesque campanile. Sadly, new construction, not only on the valley floor but up on the vineyard slopes, is gradually destroying it. Not far from Negrar is the Villa Rizzardi, set in one of the most splendid gardens of the region. It was designed in 1780 by Luigi Trezza and includes such features as a green theatre, as well as more standard elements like pools and cypress-lined avenues.

From Negrar continue south to Pedemonte. Just west of Pedemonte is Palladio's Villa Santa Sofia, one of his most eccentric works. The villa is hard to find, but if you follow the signs for the winery of the same name, you will find yourself behind the villa, and the door into the courtyard may be open. It is worth making some effort to peek at the villa, because, although only half completed, it is a unique building. The back of the mansion is relatively plain, but the courtyard is faced on three sides by two-storey loggias carried on heavily rusticated columns, a balustrade dividing the two storeys. This burly structure, like a theatre in the round, is built of rich buff-coloured stone. The rustication is uneven and deliberately coarse, as

though a beast with jaws of steel had nibbled at the columns, and this gives the courtyard its almost barbaric character.

Continue towards Verona, and skirt the northern edge of the town. Just east of Verona, take the road north towards Quinto and bear right for Santa Maria in Stelle. Alongside the church is a subterranean nymphaeum from Roman times known as the Pantheon. One of the rooms contains frescoes dating from the fifth century. At time of writing, the Pantheon was 'closed for restoration'. Return to the main road north, and just before Grezzana, in Cuzzano, you'll see on the left, set in a lovely park, the balustraded and stylishly ornamented seventeenth-century Villa Allegri-Arvedi (also called Villa Cuzzano) designed by Giovan Battista Bianchi. Curiously, two slender towers are placed at the end of terraces on either side of the house. The gardens are probably the estate's finest feature, and some elements, such as the box parterre, are contemporaneous with the villa. In Grezzana, the church has a romanesque campanile of white, pink and yellow stone. The choir stalls are elaborately inlaid, though the renaissance workmanship is not of the highest. The font displays crude but vigorous romanesque carving.

Return towards Verona, then, just outside the city, bear left towards Montorio, dominated by the ruined towers of the Scaliger castle. Head south to the main road and make for Verona. Just south of the main road in the suburb of San Michele Extra is the church of Madonna di Campagna, a circular building with a wide colonnade sweeping around it. The church is octagonal inside, with a gallery around the drum, but the choir, reached through a short barrel-vaulted passage, is domed with a barrel-vaulted apse, in which is placed the frescoed image of the Madonna. This dramatic design has been attributed to Sammicheli. The best altar-piece is Felice Brusasorci's *Deposition* of 1596.

From here it is only three kilometres to the city gates of Verona, a city to which it is always a pleasure to return, with its marvellous churches and works of art, its fine restaurants, its stylish shops, and its constant love of festivity. To return to Verona is to encounter once again the very best that the Veneto has to offer.

The showy seventeenth-century Villa Allegri-Arvedi overlooks the main road between Verona and Grezzana.

Index